Cal-a-Vie
LIVING

gourmet spa cuisine

Cal-a-Vie
LIVING
gourmet spa cuisine

Published by Cal-a-Vie, The Spa Havens
Copyright 2007 by
Cal-a-Vie, The Spa Havens
29402 Spa Havens Way, Vista, California 92084
760-945-2055

www.cal-a-vie.com

Executive Chef: Steve Pernetti
Sous Chef: Jason Graham
Photography © by Jerry Ward except as noted below
Page 8 Photograph © by Dominique Vorillon
Page 32 Photograph © by Amy Fellows
Page 55 Photograph © by Doug Hill
Editors: Terri Havens and Colleen McLeod
Contributors: Mario Guillen; Ileen Miller, MHS; Richard Yannette and Simone Rathle
Nutritional analysis provided by Cal-a-Vie
All photography shot at Cal-a-Vie Health Spa

Library of Congress Control Number: 2005937832
ISBN: 978-0-9766222-0-8

Edited, Designed, and Manufactured by **Favorite Recipes® Press**
An imprint of

FRP

P.O. Box 305142
Nashville, Tennessee 37230
800-358-0560

Art Director: Steve Newman
Book Design: Sheri Ferguson
Managing Editor: Mary Cummings
Project Manager: Tanis Westbrook
Project Editor: Jane Hinshaw

Printed in China
First Printing 2007
30,000 copies

table of contents

A TASTE OF CAL-A-VIE

We consider it our responsibility to create a cozy home-away-from-home environment at Cal-a-Vie, where guests can relax and be who they are at their happiest. People who visit Cal-a-Vie are on a mission . . . they want a peaceful and tranquil place to retreat from the world in order to focus on health, nutrition, and achieving a proper balance in their lives. That has been our mission—to create such a place, and thankfully the world has taken notice. In fact, the readers of *Travel & Leisure Magazine* just voted us #2 in its annual survey of the "Top Destination Spas in the World."

If you walk into the Cal-a-Vie kitchen before a meal, you will see a giant information board, plates and notes all personalized to the guests particular caloric intake and food allergies. This represents the overall philosophy of Cal-a-Vie . . . to help people achieve the proper balance in their lives in a very personalized one-on-one manner. Food, fitness, spirituality, pampering, and wellness are all an important part of the life. Guests have the opportunity to enjoy all of them in the manner that is most beneficial for them.

Welcome to Cal-a-Vie

Guests arriving at Cal-a-Vie drive up the private, winding road, cross a large wooden bridge spanning a running stream, and then quickly realize they have entered another world. Cal-a-Vie, The Spa Havens is situated on two hundred acres of rolling terrain blanketed with wildflowers and dramatic stands of oak and olive trees. The beauty of the surrounding landscape combined with the rustic elegance of the twenty-four Mediterranean-style villas brings to mind a Provençal village. Beauty from the natural environment is deliberately integrated into the design to enhance and heighten the effects of both the therapeutic and fitness programs. A soothing pond with running water simulates a natural spring; boulders from the foothills around the property are placed in groups, offering a sense of stability and meditative calm. A lovely garden terraced into the southern face of the property and a northern panorama of farm-dotted hills and majestic mountains in the distance add to the picture-perfect view. Life is undoubtedly different here.

The Setting

The sun-drenched sanctuary that is Cal-a-Vie may look like an age-old village in southern France, but don't let that charming patina fool you—over the past few years our luxury spa has been completely renovated inside and out.

Guests are assigned to one of the twenty-four private villas, each with either a sun deck or balcony that opens onto a breathtaking mountain view. The newly renovated villas are individually decorated with imported chintzes, charming floral prints, and linen toile of centuries-old designs. French antiques and hand-carved furnishings grace each villa, and down comforters and pillows, also covered in toile, cover each king-size bed. Comfort is paramount . . . elegance is our added pleasure.

The Schedule

The day begins early at Cal-a-Vie. Rise shortly after 6 a.m., and begin the day with stretching in preparation for a healthy workout. A hike through the hills surrounding the two-hundred-acre property or a vigorous two-mile walk around the golf course gets the blood flowing. A brief "Fit Talk" by a member of the fitness staff puts guests right in the mood for the great day ahead.

Mornings are spent in the new Fitness Center—a seventeen-thousand square-foot facility filled with the colors, light, and antique furnishings of southern France. The lobby, a soaring two-story tower with clerestory windows and a large arched doorway has antique terra-cotta flooring brought over from France, Venetian plastered walls, and a water fountain with a nine-foot-high tile back-splash imported from an old Portuguese

manor. Another wall features pale blue eighteenth-century French paneling and a stone sink with a purified waterspout. Three spacious exercise rooms contain the finest machines and equipment and covered decks and patios accommodate outdoor classes.

Afternoons are typically devoted to spa treatments and guests find themselves in The Bath House—a luxurious environment inspired by ancient Mediterranean, Turkish, and Roman baths. The Bath House has a tranquil, restful, and nurturing atmosphere filled with stones, tiles, and antique furniture.

The Food

Proper nutrition is fundamental to maintaining a healthy lifestyle, and Cal-a-Vie's culinary team takes its mission very seriously to provide guests with a dietary program that energizes the body while still being flavorful. For example, our guests can indulge in savory pizza and chocolate ice cream cake—Cal-a-Vie style that is!

Chef Steve Pernetti is the culinary chef here, with Jason Graham as his sous-chef. There is not one cultural influence to their style of cuisine. They prefer to take you on a culinary journey around the world and have you explore the many flavors of countries that inspire most chefs today.

The culinary team of Cal-a-Vie is committed to a modern approach of the low-fat, low-sodium regimen, which is high in natural complex carbohydrates (whole grains, legumes, fresh vegetables, and fruit) and includes modest amounts of lean animal proteins (dairy, egg whites, poultry, and fish) and sparing amounts of natural cold-pressed oils to complement the cuisine. A low-calorie adaptation of the classical gourmet tradition, Pernetti creatively adds fresh herbs, pepper, and lemon juice to put back the flavor and pizzazz lost from removing oil and butter.

Mealtimes at Cal-a-Vie are the "pièce de résistance" of the day, and the food philosophy here focuses on satisfaction versus portion control. Guests anxiously congregate in the mornings to see the posted menu of what will be tantalizing their taste buds throughout the day. Knowing what is on the menu of the day may determine the strength of your workouts. Early morning hikes often go by just a little bit quicker as guests look forward to a breakfast of Lourdes' Huevos Rancheros, Cal-a-Vie's famous Homemade Granola with Warm Apple Compote, or Frittata Provençal. In between workouts and treatments you will find seasoned vegetables, warm revitalizer drinks, fresh fruit and sparkling lemon water available.

Lunch is also a coveted meal—usually served alfresco, with terrycloth robe-clad guests lounging delightedly after a morning's worth of workouts. The reward? Shrimp Stack, a shrimp, mango, and avocado tower with goat cheese crouton, or Macadamia-Crusted Apple-Stuffed Duck with Sweet-and-Sour Red Cabbage, or maybe Roasted Tenderloin of Beef with Cabernet Sauce and Lobster Mashed Potatoes might be the selection of the day. The food here definitely tastes too good to be true!

After a long day of exercise and pampering, dinner can be served in the privacy of a guest's villa or in the main dining room. Chef Pernetti tantalizes your taste buds at night, serving Salmon "Egg Roll," Rigatoni alla Bolognese with Roasted Mushrooms and Ricotta Cheese, or Hoisin-Crusted Mahi Mahi and Wasabi Mashed Potatoes. Guests often proclaim that they want to take Pernetti home with them so they can eat like this every day.

And can you imagine that at nearly every meal guests at Cal-a-Vie even get dessert? At first you feel like a kid who opened the cookie jar when no one was looking, but actually anyone can look at you having a sweet, as you earned the treat. Maple Vanilla Bean Flan, Mixed Berries in Phyllo Nests, Petite Cal-a-Vie Cheesecake, Silken Chocolate Mousse, Apple Phyllo Strudel with Cinnamon Cream, and Piña Colada Sorbet are some of Chef Steve's low-fat desserts.

A highlight of the week is the Tuesday and Friday night hands-on cooking demonstration with Chef Pernetti. Guests gather in Pernetti's studio—the kitchen—and learn the art of healthy cooking right in the midst of all the action. Surrounded by gleaming metal appliances and countertops, the cacophony of pots and pans at work, and tempted by the aroma wafting from the ovens and stovetops, guests can learn the tricks of the trade while watching Chef Pernetti work

his magic with each dish—maximizing flavor while losing the fat. Customized recipe booklets are given to each participant so that guests can return home and get cooking without abandoning their newfound healthy ways.

Chef Pernetti's team are all-stars at Cal-a-Vie and their fans simply can't get over one of the most inspired culinary masterpieces. The pizza that is served on Saturdays has diners hard-pressed to believe it is "diet." That is the response to much of the food served at Cal-a-Vie. It is flavorful, tasty, and unbelievably satisfying and everyone wants to know the secret to how it is achieved. Dining at Cal-a-Vie is all about having a glorious meal and never feeling as if you have to miss out on anything.

But perhaps most important of all is the fact that Cal-a-Vie's meals really are calorie-conscious. In an undercover mission to test the food at some of the nation's top spas, *The Wall Street Journal* visited Cal-a-Vie and remarked that it was "one of our best spas for weight watchers."

The Cookbook

While we have recently made a number of the foods we serve available for guests to take home, we thought the next logical step would be for us to create a new cookbook—the culmination of thirteen years of Chef Pernetti's culinary team's creations for Cal-a-Vie guests to use at home. Since the menu changes every week and not one dish is duplicated at his cooking classes, Chef Pernetti definitely had an armful of recipes to create a fabulous healthy eating cookbook!

The recipes are the simple, no-nonsense dishes served at Cal-a-Vie and include many of the most requested favorites including the Revitalizer drink, the Homemade Granola, Chocolate Fondue, High Fiber Seed Bread, and Shrimp Spring Rolls.

We hope that this cookbook becomes your daily food bible—the binding well-worn, the corners folded down on your personal favorites, and the pages stained from continual use. It is one of the best ways in which we can help you take Cal-a-Vie home with you and to truly believe that simple, healthy eating can easily be elevated to gourmet status! This makes it easy to go home and continue "Cal-a-Vie Living."

To your health!

Terri Havens

John Havens

nutritional philosophy and guidelines

Proper nutrition plays an integral role in helping one achieve personal health and fitness goals. Cal-a-Vie has developed a menu that not only nourishes according to these principles, but also strives to instill within each guest the idea that simple, healthy eating can be indeed elevated to gourmet status. The commitment to freshness and quality, to beauty in plate presentation, and to the highest nutritional values combine to feed not only the body, but the palate and visual senses as well.

"Cal-a-Vie Cuisine" maximizes the benefits of the spa's beauty and fitness regimen. This gourmet cuisine is highlighted by garden fresh herbs, vegetables, and fruits, which are carefully prepared and artfully presented to help slim, balance, and revitalize your body, while meeting your unique nutritional needs.

The nutritional philosophy that underlies the dietary program at Cal-a-Vie reflects the latest research and understanding among health and nutrition experts—a low-fat, low-sodium diet, high in fiber, natural complex carbohydrates (approximately 50-60% of the diet for active guests) in the form of whole grains, legumes, fresh vegetables, and fruit; combined with modest amounts of lean animal proteins (approximately 25-30% of the diet) such as dairy, egg whites, poultry, and fish, plus small amounts of heart-healthy oils/fats (approximately 25-30% of the diet) that are natural, cold-pressed, and fundamental to enhanced health and longevity of the heart.

Sous Chef Jason Graham

The menus and foods are regularly analyzed for over 155 different nutrients including the percentages of fats, proteins, and carbohydrates. Steve Pernetti, the head chef, and his staff work closely with the nutritionist in the creation and modifications of the recipes. The Cal-a-Vie dining experience and this cookbook reflect this creativity and nutritional philosophy.

Executive Chef Steve Pernetti

week one

Cal-a-Vie is nestled on two hundred acres among rolling hills in a secluded valley forty miles north of San Diego, where the climate is considered to be the best in the country. At Cal-a-Vie you will discover an island in time, an exquisite oasis sheltered from the rush and competition of daily life. This is a retreat where you can relax in beautiful, natural surroundings and attain a new vitality. It is an intimate and luxurious retreat where all your needs—body, mind, and spirit—are considered and cared for by a staff committed to excellence and service.

The atmosphere at Cal-a-Vie is one of rustic elegance, where the vibrant and colorful natural landscape accentuates the comfortable and inviting appointments of the Mediterranean-style villas. The spa's architectural and interior design was created to harmonize with the environment and achieve an atmosphere of peace and tranquility. The natural beauty surrounds you, enhancing your weeklong experience of vigorous physical activity and rejuvenating beauty treatments.

Enjoy the Cal-a-Vie experience, an interlude dedicated entirely to you. In an environment of peace and beauty, those interested in health and vitality will be inspired to make positive changes in their attitudes and lifestyles and to find the path to a higher and healthier relationship with both the mind and the body.

sunday menu

Dimanche

breakfast

Whole Wheat Boysenberry Pancakes

Pure Maple Syrup

lunch

Roasted Seitan, Wehani Rice and Chilean Grape Salad

with Tarragon Vinaigrette

Kabocha Squash Sorbet

hors d'oeuvre

Roasted Eggplant Dip

Corn Chips

dinner

Roasted Tomato and Red Pepper Soup

with Lump Crab Meat Crouton

Salmon "Egg Roll"

dessert

Apple Phyllo Strudel

Cinnamon Cream

Whole Wheat Boysenberry Pancakes

1   Combine the honey, milk, almond oil and vanilla in a mixing bowl and mix well. Beat in the egg yolks. Sift the flour, baking powder, baking soda, ginger and salt into a bowl; make a well in the center. Pour the milk mixture into the well and mix just until blended. Fold in the beaten egg whites and then fold in the boysenberries gently.

2   Heat a griddle over medium heat. Oil the griddle lightly and spoon the batter 2 ounces at a time onto the griddle. Reduce the heat to medium-low and cook the pancakes until the bottom is golden brown and the top is bubbly. Turn the pancakes over and cook until golden brown on the other side. Repeat with the remaining batter.

3   Serve with pure maple syrup, a dollop of vanilla yogurt and fresh fruit.

Yields 20 (2-ounce) pancakes

1 tablespoon honey or brown sugar

2 cups 2% milk or buttermilk

1 tablespoon almond oil or canola oil

1 teaspoon vanilla extract

2 egg yolks, lightly beaten

2 cups whole wheat pastry flour

2 teaspoons baking powder

1/2 teaspoon baking soda

2 teaspoons ginger

1/4 teaspoon salt (optional)

4 egg whites, stiffly beaten

1 1/2 cups fresh or frozen boysenberries

maple syrup, vanilla yogurt and fruit

nutrition per serving

CAL	CARB	PRO	FAT	FIBER	CHOL	SOD
85	12g	4g	2g	2g	22mg	60mg

Seitan is a high-protein food made from wheat gluten, and can be purchased already roasted. Gluten is the stretchy, high-protein portion of hard winter wheat processed in such a way as to remove much of the starch. Seitan has a meaty look and texture and is featured as vegetarian "mock duck" in Asian dishes.

Roasted Seitan, Wehani Rice and Chilean Grape Salad with Tarragon Vinaigrette

Tarragon Vinaigrette

2 shallots, chopped

2 garlic cloves, chopped

1 teaspoon Dijon mustard

1 teaspoon low-sodium soy sauce

$1/4$ cup filtered water

$1/4$ cup white sherry vinegar or
   tarragon vinegar

$1/2$ teaspoon xanthan gum

1 tablespoon extra-virgin olive oil

salt and freshly ground pepper to taste

2 tablespoons chopped fresh tarragon

Salad

3 cups roasted seitan, cut into thin strips

3 cups cooked wehani rice

3 cups Chilean grapes, cut into halves

1 cup chopped celery

$1/4$ cup minced parsley

$1/4$ cup chopped chives

$1/4$ cup toasted walnuts, chopped

9 cups shredded butter lettuce

12 large butter lettuce leaves

1 For the vinaigrette, combine the shallots, garlic, Dijon mustard, soy sauce, water, vinegar and xanthan gum in a blender; process until puréed. Add the olive oil, salt and pepper gradually, processing constantly until smooth. Combine with the tarragon in a bowl and mix well.

2 For the salad, combine the seitan, wehani rice, grapes, celery, parsley and chives in a bowl. Add the shredded lettuce and vinaigrette and toss to coat evenly. Add the walnuts. Spoon the mixture onto a bed of the butter lettuce leaves.

Yield 12 servings

nutrition per serving

CAL	CARB	PRO	FAT	FIBER	CHOL	SOD
236	24g	18g	9g	2g	0mg	214mg

16

week one sunday

Kabocha Squash Sorbet

2³/₄ cups cooked kabocha squash,
    about 2 pounds fresh squash

¹/₂ cup sliced banana,
    about 1 banana

3 cups fresh orange juice

¹/₄ cup fresh lime juice

1 tablespoon orange liqueur (optional)

¹/₃ cup Splenda or stevia

1 tablespoon grated orange zest

¹/₄ teaspoon ground cinnamon

lemon, lime or orange blossoms,
    for garnish

1 Combine the squash, banana, orange juice, lime juice and orange liqueur in a blender and process until smooth. Add the Splenda, orange zest and cinnamon and process until well mixed.

2 Spoon the mixture into a freezer-safe container with sides 2 inches deep. Freeze for 8 hours or longer. Scoop with an ice cream scoop as for shaving ice. Garnish each serving with a fragrant lemon, lime or orange blossom. A crisp wafer cookie goes perfectly with this sorbet.

Yields 12 servings

nutrition per serving

CAL	CARB	PRO	FAT	FIBER	CHOL	SOD
52	12g	1g	<1g	1g	0mg	1mg

Roasted Eggplant Dip

2 large eggplant

2 tablespoons fresh lemon juice

2 tablespoons tahini (sesame seed paste)

1 teaspoon chopped garlic

1 tablespoon honey

1 teaspoon olive oil

1 teaspoon cumin

1 teaspoon coriander

pinch of salt

¹/₄ teaspoon pepper

1 Preheat the oven to 400 degrees. Cut the eggplant into halves lengthwise. Place cut side down on a baking sheet and bake for 30 minutes or until tender. Remove and discard the skins.

2 Combine the eggplant with the lemon juice, tahini, garlic, honey, olive oil, cumin, coriander, salt and pepper in a food processor. Process until smooth. Serve with vegetables or corn chips for dipping.

Yields 20 servings

nutrition per serving

CAL	CARB	PRO	FAT	FIBER	CHOL	SOD
28	4g	1g	1g	1g	0mg	2mg

This popular soup can also be made with yellow tomatoes and bell peppers, or half-and-half. Serve it with a mini grilled cheese sandwich. Fresh basil or a sprinkle of Parmesan cheese tops it off.

Roasted Tomato and Red Pepper Soup with Lump Crab Crouton

Soup

4 large red bell peppers

4 large tomatoes

2 tablespoons pomace olive oil

1/4 cup chopped yellow onion

1/4 cup unbleached flour

4 cups (or more) roasted chicken broth or
   regular chicken broth

3/4 cup (6 ounces) light coconut milk

salt and pepper to taste

Lump Crab Meat Crouton

8 ounces lump crab meat, picked for shells

1 teaspoon finely chopped shallot

2 tablespoons chopped fresh basil

1 teaspoon extra-virgin olive oil

1/2 teaspoon white truffle oil (optional)

6 (1/4-×2-inch) slices baguette, toasted

1 For the soup, preheat the oven to 450 degrees. Coat the bell peppers and tomatoes with 1 tablespoon of the olive oil and place on a baking sheet. Roast for 20 to 30 minutes or until the skin breaks away. Remove the stems from the peppers.

2 Combine the remaining 1 tablespoon olive oil with the onion, bell peppers and tomatoes in a medium saucepan. Sweat over low heat for 2 to 3 minutes. Add the flour and stir to coat well. Stir in the chicken broth and coconut milk.

3 Simmer for 20 to 30 minutes, adding additional broth if needed and stirring occasionally. Process the mixture in a blender until smooth. Strain through a regular sieve and season with salt and pepper to taste. Return to the saucepan and keep warm.

4 For the crouton, combine the crab meat, shallot, basil, olive oil and truffle oil in a small bowl and mix well. Spread on the croutons.

5 Ladle the soup into soup bowls and top each serving with a crouton. Serve with basil oil.

Yields 6 servings

nutrition per serving						
CAL	CARB	PRO	FAT	FIBER	CHOL	SOD
170	18g	14g	5g	1g	35mg	444mg

Salmon "Egg Roll"

1/4 cup light soy sauce

2 tablespoons mirin (sweet rice wine)

1 teaspoon sesame oil

1/4 teaspoon finely chopped fresh ginger

1/4 teaspoon finely chopped garlic

1/4 teaspoon finely chopped shallot

1/2 teaspoon sambal (chili sauce)

4 (3-ounce) salmon fillets

4 large egg roll wrappers

1 tablespoon vegetable oil

4 tablespoons Maple Soy Reduction (below)

1   Preheat the oven to 450 degrees. Combine soy sauce, mirin, sesame oil, ginger, garlic, shallot and sambal in a bowl and mix well. Add the salmon and marinate for 30 minutes or longer; drain.

2   Arrange the egg roll wrappers on a flat work surface and place 1 salmon fillet on each wrapper. Brush the edges of the wrappers with water and roll to enclose the salmon, pressing the edges to seal.

3   Heat the oil in a nonstick ovenproof sauté pan and add the salmon rolls. Sauté until golden brown on all sides. Bake for 8 to 10 minutes or until cooked through. Slice the rolls diagonally and stand the slices at an angle to each other on serving plates. Drizzle with the maple soy reduction.

Yields 4 servings

nutrition per serving						
CAL	CARB	PRO	FAT	FIBER	CHOL	SOD
272	21g	20g	11g	1g	50mg	1121mg

Maple Soy Reduction

2 cups pure maple syrup

1 3/4 cups light soy sauce

1/2 cup veal demi-glace or chicken
demi-glace (optional)

1   Combine the maple syrup and soy sauce in a medium saucepan. Cook until thickened enough to coat the back of a spoon. Stir in the demi-glace. Let stand until cool. Store in the refrigerator for up to 1 month.

Yields 32 (1-tablespoon) servings

nutrition per serving						
CAL	CARB	PRO	FAT	FIBER	CHOL	SOD
53	13g	0g	0g	0g	0mg	800mg

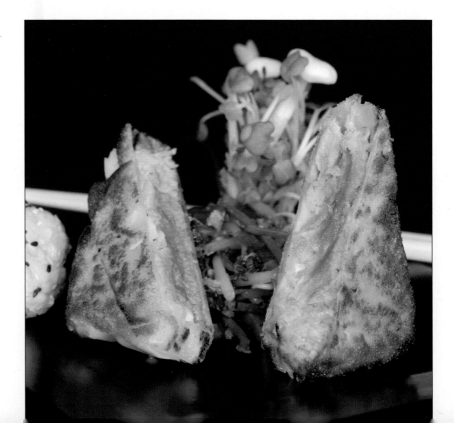

For Cinnamon Cream, combine 1/2 package extra-fine silken tofu, 1 teaspoon almond oil, 1/4 cup pure maple syrup, 2 tablespoons Splenda and 1 teaspoon cinnamon in a blender and process at high speed until smooth. Chill in the refrigerator for 1 hour.

Yields 12 (1-tablespoon) servings

nutrition per serving						
CAL	CARB	PRO	FAT	FIBER	CHOL	SOD
31	5g	1g	1g	1<g	0mg	10mg

Apple Phyllo Strudel

1 Preheat the oven to 350 degrees. Combine the apples, dried cranberries, brown sugar and cinnamon in a saucepan and cook for about 10 minutes or until tender. Let stand for 10 minutes to cool.

2 Layer 2 sheets of the phyllo on a work surface and spray with nonstick cooking spray; sprinkle with cookie crumbs. Repeat the layers 2 times with the remaining sheets. Spread the apple mixture over the phyllo. Roll the phyllo from the 12-inch side to enclose the filling.

3 Place the roll on a baking sheet sprayed with nonstick cooking spray. Bake for 25 minutes. Cool for 10 minutes before slicing to serve. Arrange on serving plates.

4 Serve with vanilla yogurt or frozen vanilla yogurt and top with the mint and raspberries. You may also serve with Cinnamon Cream (above).

Yields 12 servings

6 green apples, peeled, cored and sliced
   (about 2 pounds apples)

1/2 cup cried cranberries or dried cherries
   (about 2 1/2 ounces)

1/2 cup packed brown sugar

1 teaspoon cinnamon

6 (12×16-inch) sheets phyllo dough

butter-flavored nonstick cooking spray, or
   a mixture of 1 teaspoon melted butter
   and 1 teaspoon almond oil

1/2 cup amaretti crumbs or
   graham cracker crumbs

12 ounces nonfat vanilla yogurt or
   frozen vanilla yogurt

12 mint sprigs

36 raspberries

nutrition per serving						
CAL	CARB	PRO	FAT	FIBER	CHOL	SOD
167	37g	3g	2g	3g	1mg	91mg

monday menu

breakfast

Frittata Provençal
Toast Points and Fresh Fruit

lunch

Shrimp Stack
Fresh Fruit Smoothie

hors d'oeuvre

Vegetable Wheat Quesadilla

dinner

Mixed Greens with Fuji Apple, Walnuts
and Roasted Beets
Macadamia-Crusted Chicken Breast
with White Asparagus and Port Sauce
Butternut Squash Risotto

dessert

Mixed Berries in Phyllo Nests
with Mango Mousse

Frittata Provençal

1 Preheat the oven to 300 degrees. Beat the eggs and egg whites in a bowl until smooth. Spray an ovenproof nonstick sauté pan with nonstick cooking spray and heat over low heat. Add the eggs and cook until set; remove from heat.

2 Spread the Spa Pesto over the frittata and sprinkle with the sun-dried tomatoes, mushrooms, pine nuts and cheese. Place in the oven and bake, uncovered, for 4 minutes. Sprinkle with salt and pepper and drizzle with the olive oil. Cut into wedges and serve with toast points and fresh fruit.

Yields 4 servings

4 eggs

4 egg whites

1 tablespoon Spa Pesto (below)

^{1}/4 cup julienned rehydrated
   sun-dried tomatoes

^{1}/2 cup cooked mushrooms

1 tablespoon toasted pine nuts

2 tablespoons crumbled low-fat feta cheese

salt and pepper to taste

1 teaspoon extra-virgin olive oil

nutrition per serving						
CAL	CARB	PRO	FAT	FIBER	CHOL	SOD
187	7g	14g	12g	2g	216mg	394mg

Spa Pesto

Combine the basil, garlic, olive oil, vegetable stock, salt and pepper in a blender. Process until smooth. Store in the refrigerator.

Makes 1^1/2 cups

2 cups fresh basil leaves

1 teaspoon chopped garlic

1 teaspoon olive oil

^{1}/2 cup vegetable stock, chicken stock
   or water

salt and pepper to taste

nutrition per serving						
CAL	CARB	PRO	FAT	FIBER	CHOL	SOD
105	2g	9g	7g	1g	144mg	161mg

week one monday

Shrimp Stack

12 large shrimp, cleaned and poached

2 avocados, chopped

2 large tomatoes, chopped

1 mango, chopped

4 scallions, thinly sliced

1 jalapeño chile, seeded and
   minced (optional)

leaves of 1 bunch fresh cilantro

2 tablespoons fresh lemon juice

salt and pepper to taste

cilantro sprigs, for garnish

1 Cut the shrimp into halves and combine with the avocados, tomatoes, mango, scallions and jalapeño chile in a medium bowl. Add the cilantro and lemon juice; season with salt and pepper and toss to mix well.

2 Pack the mixture into molds or plastic cups and chill in the refrigerator. Invert onto serving plates and garnish with cilantro sprigs. Serve with large croutons.

3 You may add tabouli or legumes to the stack for added carbohydrates; alternative protein sources work just as well.

4 You may add chopped peeled kiwifruit to the stack if desired.

Yields 4 servings

nutrition per serving						
CAL	CARB	PRO	FAT	FIBER	CHOL	SOD
215	22g	7g	13g	9g	32mg	49mg

Fresh Fruit Smoothie

8 ounces frozen strawberries

1 cup sliced peaches

2 blackberries

1 cup apple juice

1 teaspoon flax seed oil

1 scoop vanilla protein powder

2 teaspoons Splenda or honey (optional)

3 strawberries, cut into halves, for garnish

6 pineapple wedges, for garnish

1 Combine the strawberries, peaches and blackberries in a blender. Add the apple juice, flax seed oil, protein powder and Splenda. Process at high speed for 1 minute, adding additional juice if the smoothie is too thick or additional berries if it is too thin.

2 Pour into chilled glasses and garnish with a strawberry half and a pineapple wedge.

Yields 6 servings

nutrition per serving						
CAL	CARB	PRO	FAT	FIBER	CHOL	SOD
64	13g	2g	1g	2g	3mg	4mg

For a higher protein snack or entrée, add cooked lean steak, chicken, or shrimp to the quesadilla before baking.

Vegetable Wheat Quesadilla

2 sprouted wheat tortillas

1 cup (4 ounces) shredded part-skim-milk
   mozzarella cheese

1/2 cup sliced mushrooms

1 teaspoon vegetable oil

salt and pepper to taste

1/2 cup julienned zucchini

1/4 cup finely chopped green onions

pico de gallo (optional)

1   Preheat the oven to 400 degrees. Place 1 of the tortillas on a work surface and sprinkle with the cheese. Sauté the mushrooms in the oil in a skillet over high heat until tender. Sprinkle with salt and pepper. Spread over the cheese.

2   Sauté the zucchini in the same skillet. Spread the zucchini and green onions over the mushrooms; sprinkle with salt and pepper. Top with the remaining tortilla and press down lightly.

3   Place on a baking sheet sprayed lightly with nonstick cooking spray. Bake for 12 to 15 minutes or until the cheese melts and the quesadilla is heated through. Cut into 8 wedges. Serve with pico de gallo.

Yields 8 servings

nutrition per serving						
CAL	CARB	PRO	FAT	FIBER	CHOL	SOD
71	6g	5g	4g	1g	8mg	118mg

Mixed Greens with Fuji Apple, Walnuts and Roasted Beets

1 Preheat the oven to 400 degrees. Arrange the beets on a baking sheet, and roast for 30 minutes or until the skins peel easily. Let stand until cool. Peel the beets.

2 Toss the walnuts and Splenda together in a nonstick skillet coated with butter-flavor nonstick cooking spray. Cook over medium heat for a few minutes or until the walnuts are coated.

3 Combine the beets, walnuts, mixed greens, apple and shallot in a large bowl. Add the vinegar and olive oil and toss to coat well. Sprinkle with the cheese and season with salt and pepper. Serve immediately.

Yields 6 servings

10 red or yellow beets

2 tablespoons chopped walnuts

1 tablespoon Splenda

6 cups washed and dried mixed
   baby greens

1 Fuji apple, chopped

1 large shallot, chopped

3 tablespoons balsamic vinegar

1 teaspoon extra-virgin olive oil

2 tablespoons crumbled blue cheese

salt and pepper to taste

nutrition per serving						
CAL	CARB	PRO	FAT	FIBER	CHOL	SOD
81	9g	3g	4g	2g	4mg	116mg

At Cal-a-Vie, we always dress a salad at the last possible second for a crisp and fresh look. You can use any type of apple, but we prefer a Fuji or other sweet apple, skin and all. This salad also is a perfect starter for herb-crusted sea bass or rack of lamb.

week one monday

This is a good protein-rich dish for the more advanced home cook. The presentation is visually pleasing when the chicken is sliced and fanned in a pinwheel over or beside the risotto, with the sauce spooned around the edge. For a version lower in fat, replace the macadamia crust with an herb crust.

Macadamia-Crusted Chicken

Port Sauce

2 cups port

4 sprigs of parsley, chopped

2 large shallots, chopped

1 teaspoon black peppercorns

1 cup veal demi-glace or chicken demi-glace

salt and pepper to taste

Macadamia Crust

2 ounces toasted macadamia nuts

3/4 cup panko (Japanese bread crumbs)

1 teaspoon vegetable oil

1 teaspoon Splenda

salt and white pepper to taste

1/2 teaspoon curry powder

1/4 cup cilantro

Chicken

4 (6-ounce) boneless skinless chicken
   breasts with tenderloins

2 cups cooked wild mushrooms, cooled

2 tablespoons light coconut milk

1 egg

salt and pepper to taste

1 bunch white asparagus

1 egg, beaten

1 For the sauce, combine the wine, parsley, shallots and peppercorns in a small saucepan. Cook until reduced by half. Add the demi-glace and cook until reduced to a thick consistency. Season with salt and pepper and set aside.

2 For the macadamia crust, process the macadamia nuts in a food processor until mealy. Add the bread crumbs, oil and Splenda; season with salt and white pepper to taste. Process until mixed. Add the curry powder and cilantro and pulse until the cilantro is chopped.

3 For the chicken, preheat the oven to 450 degrees. Remove the tenderloins from the breasts. Combine the tenderloins with the mushrooms in a food processor and process until puréed. Add the coconut milk, 1 egg and salt and pepper to taste. Pulse 20 times or until combined. Blanch the asparagus in salted water in a saucepan; drain.

4 Pound the remaining chicken between 2 sheets of plastic wrap until flattened. Spoon the puréed mushroom mixture in a thin 1/2-inch-thick strip across the width of the chicken. Arrange the asparagus over the filling. Season with salt and pepper and roll the chicken to enclose the filling.

5 Dip the rolls in the beaten egg and roll in the macadamia crust mixture, coating well. Place on a baking sheet. Roast for 25 minutes or to 157 degrees internally; the chicken will continue to cook for several minutes after being removed from the oven and should reach an ideal internal temperature of 160 degrees.

6 Let the rolls stand for 5 minutes. Reheat the port sauce. Slice the chicken rolls and fan the slices onto 6 serving plates. Serve with the port sauce.

Yields 6 servings

nutrition per serving

CAL	CARB	PRO	FAT	FIBER	CHOL	SOD
341	20g	34g	13g	3g	137mg	298mg

Butternut Squash Risotto

8 cups (about) chicken broth

salt and white pepper to taste

1/4 cup finely chopped yellow onion

1 teaspoon pomace olive oil

2 cups uncooked arborio rice

2 tablespoons white wine

1 butternut squash,
   cooked and puréed

1/4 cup light coconut milk

1 teaspoon extra-virgin olive oil

2 teaspoons grated Parmesan cheese

2 sprigs of fresh thyme

1 Bring the chicken broth to a boil in a medium saucepan. Season with salt and white pepper. Reduce the heat and maintain the broth at a simmer.

2 Sauté the onion in the pomace olive oil in a medium saucepan for 4 minutes or until tender but not brown. Add the rice and sauté until well coated. Add the wine, stirring to deglaze the saucepan; cook until the wine evaporates.

3 Add just enough of the simmering broth to cover the rice and cook over medium heat until the broth is absorbed, stirring constantly. Repeat the process until the rice is nearly tender.

4 Add the squash purée, coconut milk, extra-virgin olive oil, cheese and thyme, and cook until the rice is tender. Refrigerate any remaining chicken broth for another use.

Yields 6 servings

nutrition per serving

CAL	CARB	PRO	FAT	FIBER	CHOL	SOD
395	67g	12g	10g	3g	1mg	920mg

The strawberries should be sliced or cut to the size of the other berries, as the more uniform fruit mixes better. Do not spoon the berries into the nests until you are ready to serve. If you are serving a liqueur with the dessert, we suggest Grand Marnier, Triple Sec or Amaretto to complement the Mango Mousse.

Mixed Berries in Phyllo Nests

1 Preheat the oven to 350 degrees. Layer 3 sheets of the phyllo dough on a work surface and cut into fourths. Pleat the pieces into muffin cups sprayed with nonstick cooking spray with the edges extending about the cups to form the nests. Repeat with the remaining phyllo dough.

2 Mix the cinnamon and confectioners' sugar in a shaker and sprinkle lightly over the nests. Bake the nests for 6 minutes or until golden brown.

3 Purée 1 cup of the strawberries in a food processor or blender; strain. Slice the remaining strawberries and combine with the blueberries, blackberries, raspberries and strawberry purée in a bowl; mix gently.

4 Spoon the berries into the phyllo nests. Top each with 2 tablespoons Mango Mousse and garnish with mint sprigs.

Yields 12 servings

9 (14×18-inch) sheets phyllo dough

1 teaspoon ground cinnamon

1 tablespoon confectioners' sugar

2 pints strawberries

1 pint blueberries

1 pint blackberries

1 pint raspberries

Mango Mousse (below)

mint sprigs, for garnish

nutrition per serving						
CAL	CARB	PRO	FAT	FIBER	CHOL	SOD
75	15g	1g	1g	2g	0mg	70mg

1 Scrape the vanilla bean into the maple syrup in a small saucepan and bring to a boil over low heat; the vanilla seeds will be released into the syrup.

2 Strain the mixture into a blender and add the mango, almond oil and Splenda; process at high speed for 1 minute or until smooth. Spoon into a bowl and chill for 2 hours.

Yields 6 (1/4-cup) servings

Mango Mousse

1 vanilla bean

1/4 cup pure maple syrup

1 very ripe mango, peeled and chopped

1 teaspoon almond oil

1 tablespoon Splenda

nutrition per serving						
CAL	CARB	PRO	FAT	FIBER	CHOL	SOD
93	21g	1g	1g	1g	0mg	11mg

a day at Cal-a-Vie

une journée

Although each guest's schedule is tailored to fit his or her specific goals and desires, below is a "sample day" of fitness, stress relief, and nutrition at Cal-a-Vie.

6:15 Morning Hike or Two-Mile Walk on the golf course: A perfect way to begin the day! These hikes include a variety of terrain, multiple types of inclines and declines, scenic vistas, luscious chaparral, and a great workout. Varying in length, the trails are among the beautiful rolling foothills that surround the spa and are all within Cal-a-Vie's spacious two-hundred plus acres.

8:00 Breakfast

8:40 "Fit Talk" with a member of the fitness staff

8:50 Warm-Up Class

9:00 Sports Conditioning: Alternating between aerobic movements that simulate training moves one might engage in when mastering a specific sport or skill and free-weight exercises, the variety of fun activities and a playful approach to this class hides how hard you are working. Different levels of intensity are continuously offered and demonstrated to allow guests of all ages and abilities to participate.

10:00 Stability Balls: Originating in the area of physical therapy for rehabilitation, these oversized balls are excellent tools for creating a variety of exercises. The ball can provide a full spectrum of exercises that will help improve core strength, overall muscle endurance, and balance.

10:50 Revitalizer

11:00 Spinning Class: This stationary bicycle journey is performed on Schwinn Elite Spinners with the "smart release breaking system," which is particularly beneficial to the beginning spinner. This workout is very rigorous, but can be tailored to all levels of fitness.

12:00 Hair and Scalp Treatment

1:00 Lunch

2:00 Seaweed Wrap

3:50 Revitalizer

4:00 Yoga Class: Classic "Hatha" yoga postures are performed and assisted. Certified instructors work closely with you to assure proper body alignment and movement precision. Breathing techniques are introduced as well as mental and relaxation exercises. This restorative yoga approach allows the body to recover from all of the demands of the hikes and other fitness classes.

5:00 Massage

6:30 Hors d'Oeuvre

7:00 Dinner

8:00 Stress Management Lecture

a day at Cal-a-Vie

tuesday menu

breakfast

Whole Grain Waffles

Maple Syrup

Fresh Fruit

lunch

Seared Ahi Tuna

Edamame and Soba Noodle Salad

Macadamia Papaya Cookies

hors d'oeuvre

Marinated Artichoke Hearts with

Roasted Red Bell Pepper Dip

dinner

Rigatoni alla Bolognese with

Roasted Mushrooms and Ricotta Cheese

dessert

Chocolate Fondue with

Seasonal Fruit

Fresh fruit, berries, or vanilla bean syrup make an excellent addition to this low-fat breakfast. You can also add fat-free whipped cream or sugar-free maple syrup. The waffles are best when served right out of the waffle iron, but if you need to reheat them, place them in the toaster for a minute.

Whole Grain Waffles

1 Combine the eggs, milk, sour cream, almond oil and vanilla in the blender. Mix the whole wheat flour, unbleached flour, baking powder, brown sugar and salt in a mixing bowl. Add the milk mixture and mix just until moistened; do not overmix.

2 Spray a waffle iron with butter-flavor nonstick cooking spray and spoon 1/3 cup of the batter at a time onto the surface. Cook using the manufacturer's directions.

Yields 6 servings

2 eggs

1 cup 1% milk

1/2 cup light sour cream

1 tablespoon almond oil or vegetable oil

1 teaspoon vanilla extract

1 cup whole wheat pastry flour

1 cup unbleached flour

1 tablespoon baking powder

1/4 cup packed brown sugar

salt to taste

nutrition per serving

CAL	CARB	PRO	FAT	FIBER	CHOL	SOD
276	44g	9g	7g	2g	81mg	404mg

week one tuesday

This dish is a great warm-weather lunch or dinner. We prefer to serve it rare to medium-rare. Since exceptionally fresh tuna is paramount, look for very firm reddish-purple flesh. We recommend you buy it at your local fish market. Request only the center portion of the fish for this dish because slicing fatty portions with uniformity can be difficult.

Seared Ahi Tuna

¹/4 cup paprika

¹/4 cup black sesame seeds

¹/4 cup white sesame seeds

2 tablespoons granulated garlic

1 teaspoon onion powder

1 teaspoon dried thyme

1 teaspoon Splenda

1 teaspoon kosher salt

2 teaspoons cayenne pepper

1 teaspoon white pepper

1 teaspoon black pepper

25 ounces fresh premium grade ahi tuna

2 tablespoons pomace olive oil

1 Mix the paprika, black sesame seeds, white sesame seeds, granulated garlic, onion powder, thyme, Splenda, kosher salt, cayenne pepper, white pepper and black pepper on a large plate.

2 Cut the tuna into 6 rectangles and coat lightly with the spice mixture. Heat the olive oil to smoking in a large nonstick sauté pan. Sear the tuna on all 4 sides, lowering the heat if necessary to avoid burning the spices.

3 Remove the tuna to a large plate and let stand for 1 minute. Cut across the grain into 1/4-inch slices. If you prefer more well done tuna, use an ovenproof pan and finish cooking the tuna in a 450-degree oven for 4 to 5 minutes.

Yields 6 servings

38

nutrition per serving						
CAL	CARB	PRO	FAT	FIBER	CHOL	SOD
209	7g	24g	8g	2g	86mg	423mg

Edamame and Soba Noodle Salad

1 Bring the water to a boil in a large saucepan and add salt and oil. Add the noodles and reduce the heat to a simmer. Cook the noodles until tender, stirring constantly. Drain the noodles and soak in ice water for 5 minutes; drain again.

2 Combine the vinegar, mirin, almond oil, ginger, garlic, shallot, chili sauce, Splenda and white pepper in a bowl and mix well. Add the noodles, edamame and wakame and toss to coat well. Chill for 30 minutes.

Yields 6 servings

1¹/2 gallons water

salt to taste

dash of vegetable oil

8 ounces uncooked buckwheat
    soba noodles

¹/2 cup unseasoned rice vinegar

¹/4 cup mirin (sweet rice wine)

2 teaspoons almond oil

1 teaspoon finely chopped fresh ginger

1 teaspoon chopped garlic

1 teaspoon chopped shallot

1 teaspoon sambal (chili sauce)

1 teaspoon Splenda

white pepper to taste

16 ounces edamame (soy beans)

3 ounces wakame (seaweed)

39

nutrition per serving						
CAL	CARB	PRO	FAT	FIBER	CHOL	SOD
325	46g	14g	8g	4g	0mg	481mg

Substitute any nut or dried fruit that you like for the ones called for in this recipe. You can substitute carob chips for the chocolate chips or omit the chocolate chips if you prefer and increase the amount of dried papaya by 3 tablespoons and the macadamia nuts by 2 tablespoons.

Macadamia Papaya Cookies

1 cup rolled oats

3/4 cup whole wheat pastry flour

1 1/2 teaspoons baking powder

1/3 cup chocolate chips

1/3 cup chopped dried papaya

1/3 cup chopped macadamia nuts

3/4 teaspoon cinnamon

1/4 teaspoon nutmeg or mace

3/4 cup mashed banana

1 egg, or 2 egg whites, lightly beaten

1/4 cup maple syrup

1 to 2 tablespoons brown sugar, or to taste

1 teaspoon vanilla extract

1 Preheat the oven to 350 degrees. Process the oats in a blender until coarsely ground. Combine the oats with the flour, baking powder, chocolate chips, dried papaya, macadamia nuts, cinnamon and nutmeg in a large bowl. Add the banana, egg, maple syrup, brown sugar and vanilla. Mix until moistened.

2 Drop by teaspoonfuls onto a cookie sheet sprayed with nonstick cooking spray. Bake for 10 to 12 minutes or until golden brown. Cool on the cookie sheet for several minutes and remove to a wire rack to cool completely.

Yields 36 (1-cookie) servings

40

nutrition per serving						
CAL	CARB	PRO	FAT	FIBER	CHOL	SOD
50	9g	1g	2g	1g	6mg	18mg

Marinated Artichoke Hearts

1 Trim the artichokes, cutting off the stems and about ¹/₂ inch of the tops. Combine with the wine and enough water to cover the artichokes in a large saucepan. Tie the bay leaves, thyme, basil and peppercorns in cheesecloth. Add the herb packet and lemons to the saucepan.

2 Place a water-filled bowl on top of the saucepan to keep the artichokes submerged. Bring the water to a boil and reduce the heat. Simmer for 45 minutes or until the artichokes are tender. Drain and cool.

Yields 12 servings

12 globe artichokes

¹/₂ cup white wine (optional)

10 cups water, or more to cover

2 bay leaves

2 tablespoons fresh thyme

2 tablespoons fresh basil

10 peppercorns

2 lemons, cut into halves

nutrition per serving

CAL	CARB	PRO	FAT	FIBER	CHOL	SOD
76	16g	5g	<1g	8g	0mg	123mg

Roasted Red Pepper Dip

1 Combine the tofu, bell peppers, garlic, shallot and capers in a blender. Add the vinegar, mayonnaise, lemon juice, Dijon mustard, kosher salt and cayenne pepper. Pulse until the mixture is chopped, using a spoon to break up the mixture between pulses. Process at high speed for 30 seconds or until smooth.

2 Serve on crab cakes or with artichokes, chips or warm bread.

Yields 16 servings

1 package silken tofu

2 roasted red bell peppers, peeled
   and seeded

1 garlic clove

1 shallot

1 teaspoon capers

2 tablespoons rice vinegar

2 tablespoons nonfat mayonnaise

1 tablespoon lemon juice

1 teaspoon Dijon mustard

kosher salt to taste

¹/₄ teaspoon cayenne pepper

nutrition per serving

CAL	CARB	PRO	FAT	FIBER	CHOL	SOD
20	2g	1g	1g	<1g	<1mg	31mg

Rigatoni alla Bolognese

2 gallons water

salt to taste

vegetable oil

1 pound fresh or dried rigatoni

1 teaspoon extra-virgin olive oil

pepper to taste

1 tablespoon basil oil (optional)

1 recipe Turkey and Tomato
   Bolognese Sauce (page 43)

1 recipe Roasted Mushrooms (page 43)

4 teaspoons low-fat ricotta cheese

4 teaspoons grated Parmigiano-Reggiano

1   Bring the water to a boil in a large stockpot. Add salt and a dash of vegetable oil. Add the pasta and cook until tender, stirring frequently; drain well.

2   Combine the pasta with the olive oil in a bowl and season with salt and pepper. Spoon into bowls dotted with basil oil and top with the Turkey Tomato Bolognese Sauce, Roasted Mushrooms, ricotta cheese and Parmigiano-Reggiano.

Yields 10 servings

nutrition per serving						
CAL	CARB	PRO	FAT	FIBER	CHOL	SOD
333	46g	19g	8g	4g	40mg	136mg

Rigatoni alla Bolognese is a Cal-a-Vie comfort food and a cooking class favorite. You can experiment with different pastas, such as ziti, penne, or ravioli. The sauce can be frozen for up to one month.

Turkey and Tomato Bolognese Sauce

1 Brown the turkey in a saucepan, stirring until crumbly. Add the onion, carrot, celery and garlic. Add the wine and cook for 2 to 3 minutes. Stir in the tomatoes, basil, parsley, thyme, salt and pepper.

2 Simmer the sauce for 30 minutes. Add the cheese and pulse with a hand-held blender until smooth. You can freeze sauce not used in the Rigatoni alla Bolognese.

Yields 6 (2-cup) servings

1 pound ground turkey

1/2 onion, chopped

1/2 cup chopped carrot

2 ribs celery, chopped

3 tablespoons minced garlic

1/2 cup red wine

2 (28-ounce) cans peeled whole tomatoes
   with basil

5 or 6 basil leaves

1/2 teaspoon chopped fresh parsley

1 tablespoon chopped fresh thyme

salt and pepper to taste

1/2 cup low-fat or light ricotta cheese

nutrition per serving

CAL	CARB	PRO	FAT	FIBER	CHOL	SOD
218	18g	18g	8g	4g	65mg	143mg

Roasted Mushrooms

1 Preheat the oven to 450 degrees. Remove the mushroom stems and reserve for another use. Brush the caps with a damp towel to clean. Do not wash the mushrooms with water, as they will become soggy. Tear the mushrooms into 1-inch pieces by hand and combine in a bowl with the shallots, garlic, olive oil, salt and pepper.

2 Spread in a single layer on a baking sheet. Roast for 15 to 20 minutes or until tender; drain. Serve immediately.

Yields 4 servings

1 cup cremini mushrooms

1 cup black trumpet mushrooms

1 cup king oyster mushrooms

1 cup chanterelle mushrooms

2 tablespoons chopped shallots

1 tablespoon crushed garlic

1 teaspoon extra-virgin olive oil

salt and pepper to taste

nutrition per serving

CAL	CARB	PRO	FAT	FIBER	CHOL	SOD
199	19g	13g	9g	5g	0mg	197mg

Ah, the universal dessert accompaniment. We think our guests wouldn't mind a large bowl of our Chocolate Fondue each day as a meal replacement. We serve it with fresh seasonal fruit, such as apples, bananas, mango, strawberries or blood oranges, but you may use the fruit of your choice.

Chocolate Fondue

1/4 cup Kahlúa

1/2 cup 1% milk

1/4 cup honey

1/2 cup baking cocoa

1 teaspoon arrowroot

1 tablespoon vanilla extract

1 Combine the Kahlúa, milk, honey, baking cocoa, arrowroot and vanilla in a saucepan and mix well. Cook over medium-low heat until thickened and smooth, stirring constantly.

2 Serve warm with bananas, strawberries or other fresh fruit for dipping.

Yields 12 servings

44

nutrition per serving						
CAL	CARB	PRO	FAT	FIBER	CHOL	SOD
56	11g	1g	1g	1g	<1mg	7mg

wednesday menu
mercredi

breakfast

Lourdes' Huevos Rancheros

Cal-a-Vie Guacamole

lunch

Wild Mushroom and Roasted Garlic Pizza

Petite Caesar Salad

Frozen Raspberry Mousse

hors d'oeuvre

Spicy Rock Shrimp Won Tons

with Roasted Cashew Dipping Sauce

dinner

Egg Drop Vegetable Soup

Hoisin-Crusted Mahi Mahi

Wasabi Mashed Potatoes

Sweet Sake Black Bean Sauce

dessert

Petite Cal-a-Vie Cheesecake

To prepare Cal-a-Vie Guacamole, peel and pit two ripe avocados, reserving the pits. Combine the avocados with two tablespoons each finely chopped onion, tomato and cilantro, two teaspoons finely chopped jalapeño chile, the juice of one lime or lemon and salt and pepper to taste in a bowl. Whisk until smooth, or leave a bit chunky, if preferred. Spoon into a bowl and serve immediately. To serve later, place the pits in the center and place plastic wrap directly on the surface of the guacamole. Store in the refrigerator.

Yields 8 servings

nutrition per serving						
CAL	CARB	PRO	FAT	FIBER	CHOL	SOD
85	5g	1g	8g	3g	0mg	9mg

Lourdes' Huevos Rancheros

1 Sauté the onion and garlic in a sauté pan sprayed with nonstick cooking spray. Add the chipotle chile, coriander, cumin and chili powder and sauté over low heat for several minutes.

2 Add the stock and bring to a boil. Cook for 5 minutes. Add the tomatoes and return to a boil. Reduce the heat and simmer until of the desired consistency. Cool for 10 minutes. Process in a blender or food processor until puréed. Combine with the cilantro and salt to taste in a bowl.

3 Cook the eggs over easy in a sauté pan sprayed with nonstick cooking spray. Slide the eggs onto the tortillas on serving plates and top with the sauce. Garnish with shredded low-fat cheese, if desired.

Yields 6 servings

1 tablespoon chopped onion

2 teaspoons chopped garlic

1 chipotle chile, chopped

1 teaspoon each coriander, cumin and chili powder

1/2 cup chicken stock or vegetable stock

1 (28-ounce) can peeled whole tomatoes

2 tablespoons chopped fresh cilantro

salt to taste

12 eggs

6 corn tortillas or whole wheat tortillas

shredded low-fat cheese, for garnish

week one wednesday

nutrition per serving						
CAL	CARB	PRO	FAT	FIBER	CHOL	SOD
356	39g	19g	14g	5g	423mg	650mg

Cal-a-Vie Wild Mushroom and Roasted Garlic Pizza

10 cremini mushrooms, sliced

1 teaspoon olive oil

1/4 cup white wine

1/4 cup mixed fresh basil, oregano and parsley

4 Roma tomatoes, thinly sliced

1 Pizza Crust (below)

1 cup (4 ounces) shredded low-fat mozzarella cheese

1 tablespoon grated asiago cheese

20 whole or coarsely chopped roasted garlic cloves

1 Preheat the oven to 500 degrees. Sauté the mushrooms in the olive oil in a sauté pan for several minutes. Add the wine and cook for several minutes. Stir in the herbs and remove from the heat.

2 Arrange the sliced tomatoes on the Pizza Crust. Sprinkle with the cheeses and top with the roasted garlic and sautéed mushrooms. Bake for 15 minutes or until the crust is golden brown. Serve with a salad of mixed greens.

3 Nutritional analysis includes the pizza crust.

Yields 4 servings

nutrition per serving						
CAL	CARB	PRO	FAT	FIBER	CHOL	SOD
353	51g	18g	9g	6g	17mg	190mg

Pizza Crusts

2 tablespoons dry yeast

1 1/2 cups warm water

2 tablespoons honey

1 tablespoon virgin olive oil

pinch of sea salt

1/2 cup semolina flour

2 1/4 cups whole wheat flour

2 1/3 cups unbleached flour

1 Mix the yeast with the water, honey, olive oil and sea salt in a bowl; let stand to activate the yeast. Mix the semolina flour, whole wheat flour and unbleached flour together. Add enough of the flour mixture to the yeast mixture to make a firm dough, kneading well.

2 Place in a lightly greased bowl, turning to coat the surface; cover with a towel. Let rise for 20 minutes or until doubled in bulk. Punch down the dough and remove to a lightly floured surface.

3 Preheat the oven to 500 degrees. Shape the dough into 3 balls. Roll into circles slightly larger than 12 inches. Place in 3 lightly oiled 12-inch pizza pans and shape raised edges. Top and bake immediately or cover with plastic wrap and store in the refrigerator until needed.

Yields 3 pizza crusts

Petite Caesar Salad

1 Combine the garlic, olive oil, lemon juice, vinegar, Pickapeppa Sauce, fish sauce, Dijon mustard and buttermilk in a bowl or blender container; mix or process until smooth.

2 Chop the romaine hearts into bite-size pieces. Combine with the dressing in a large bowl and toss to coat evenly. Season with pepper. Top each serving with 1 teaspoon Parmesan cheese and 1 1/2 teaspoons croutons.

Yields 6 servings

1 1/2 tablespoons minced garlic

1 1/2 tablespoons virgin olive oil

2 tablespoons lemon juice

2 tablespoons sherry vinegar

1 tablespoon Pickapeppa Sauce or
    Worcestershire sauce

1/2 teaspoon Thai fish sauce (optional)

1 tablespoon Dijon mustard

1/3 cup nonfat buttermilk or yogurt

hearts of 3 heads romaine

freshly cracked pepper to taste

2 tablespoons freshly grated
    Parmesan cheese

3 tablespoons dry croutons

nutrition per serving						
CAL	CARB	PRO	FAT	FIBER	CHOL	SOD
71	6g	3g	4g	2g	2mg	90mg

Frozen Raspberry Mousse

1 Combine the frozen raspberries, banana, honey, protein powder, Splenda, orange juice and vanilla in a chilled food processor. Process for 5 minutes or until the mixture is thick and smooth.

2 Spoon into 8 chilled dessert cups and serve immediately, garnished with mint and additional raspberries. You can also freeze the mixture to serve later and scoop it into the serving cups.

Yields 8 servings

3 cups frozen raspberries

3/4 ripe banana

3 tablespoons honey

1/2 cup vanilla protein powder

1/4 cup Splenda

1/4 cup fresh orange juice

1 teaspoon vanilla extract

mint sprigs, for garnish

nutrition per serving						
CAL	CARB	PRO	FAT	FIBER	CHOL	SOD
90	16g	7g	<1g	3g	0mg	73mg

Spicy Rock Shrimp Won Tons

2 teaspoons dark sesame oil

4 ounces rock shrimp

3 garlic cloves, minced

1 tablespoon minced fresh ginger

1 tablespoon curry powder (optional)

2 carrots, peeled and finely chopped

2 ribs celery, finely chopped

1 red bell pepper, finely chopped

2 cups julienned napa cabbage

8 scallions, chopped

8 water chestnuts, finely chopped (optional)

2 tablespoons rice wine vinegar

1 tablespoon low-sodium soy sauce or
   Bragg's Liquid Aminos

1 teaspoon sambal (chili sauce) or hot red
   pepper sauce

30 won ton wrappers

1 egg white, beaten

1 Preheat the oven to 350 degrees. Heat the sesame oil in a nonstick skillet. Add the shrimp and sauté until opaque. Add the garlic, ginger and curry powder. Sauté for 1 minute, stirring constantly with a wooden spoon. Add the carrots, celery, bell pepper, cabbage, scallions and water chestnuts and sauté over high heat for 1 minute.

2 Add the rice wine vinegar, soy sauce and sambal. Cook for 3 to 4 minutes or until the vegetables are seasoned and tender-crisp, stirring frequently; add a few tablespoons of soup stock if needed to prevent sticking. Strain the mixture through a stainless steel or nylon mesh strainer into a bowl, reserving the liquid for the Roasted Cashew Dipping Sauce (page 51).

3 Arrange the won ton wrappers on a work surface. Place 1 teaspoon of the shrimp mixture on 1 side of each wrapper and fold the wrappers over to enclose the filling. Brush the inner edges of the wrappers with the egg white and press the edges gently with a fork to seal. Brush the tops with the remaining egg white.

4 Place the won tons on a baking sheet sprayed with nonstick cooking spray. Bake for 15 to 20 minutes or until crisp and golden brown. You can freeze the prepared won tons and thaw to bake later. Serve with Roasted Cashew Dipping Sauce.

Yields 15 (2-won ton) servings

nutrition per won ton						
CAL	CARB	PRO	FAT	FIBER	CHOL	SOD
74	12g	4g	1g	1g	16mg	183mg

Roasted Cashew Dipping Sauce

1 Combine the cashews, jalapeño chile, garlic, scallions, ginger, mint leaves and cilantro in a blender. Add the reserved vegetable liquid from the Spicy Rock Shrimp Won Tons, the soy sauce, filtered water, mirin and rice vinegar and process until smooth.

2 Serve with Spicy Rock Shrimp Won Tons or as a sauce for steamed or fresh vegetables.

3 You may substitue 1/4 teaspoon dried mint for the fresh mint, vegetable stock or defatted chicken stock for the filtered water and Bragg's Liquid Aminos for the low-sodium soy sauce.

Yields 6 servings

2 tablespoons toasted cashews

1 jalapeño chile, seeded

2 garlic cloves, chopped

2 tablespoons chopped scallions

1 teaspoon chopped fresh ginger

2 fresh mint leaves

1 tablespoon chopped cilantro

reserved liquid from the Spicy Rock Shrimp
    Won Tons (page 50)

3 to 4 tablespoons low-sodium soy sauce

1/4 cup filtered water

1 tablespoon mirin (sweet rice wine)

2 tablespoons rice vinegar

nutrition per serving						
CAL	CARB	PRO	FAT	FIBER	CHOL	SOD
23	2g	1g	1g	<1g	<1mg	296mg

Egg Drop Vegetable Soup

1 tablespoon vegetable oil

2 tablespoons finely chopped fresh ginger

2 tablespoons finely chopped garlic

2 tablespoons finely chopped shallots

1/2 teaspoon sambal (chili sauce)

1/4 cup sake

30 ounces defatted roasted chicken stock

1 tablespoon oyster sauce

salt and white pepper to taste

2 stalks bok choy, finely chopped

2 cups assorted mushrooms,
    cut into 1/2-inch pieces

1 egg

1 egg white

1 Heat the oil in a medium saucepan over how heat. Add the ginger, garlic and shallots and sweat for 5 minutes. Add the sambal and mix well. Add the sake and stock, stirring to deglaze the saucepan. Bring to a boil and reduce the heat. Simmer for 30 minutes. Stir in the oyster sauce, salt and white pepper.

2 Strain the mixture into another saucepan and keep warm over low heat. Add the bok choy and mushrooms and bring to a simmer.

3 Beat the egg and egg white with a few drops of water in a bowl for 30 seconds. Remove the soup from the heat and stir in the egg mixture with a chopstick or fork. Let stand, covered, until ready to serve.

Yields 6 servings

nutrition per serving

CAL	CARB	PRO	FAT	FIBER	CHOL	SOD
72	5g	3g	4g	1g	36mg	481mg

Hoisin-Crusted Mahi Mahi

2 tablespoons hoisin sauce

2 tablespoons dry sherry

2 tablespoons light soy sauce

1/4 cup mirin (sweet rice wine)

1 teaspoon sambal (chili sauce)

1/2 teaspoon curry powder

1 teaspoon chopped fresh ginger

1 teaspoon chopped garlic

8 (2-ounce) pieces of mahi mahi

salt and white pepper to taste

1 Combine the hoisin sauce, sherry, soy sauce, mirin, sambal, curry powder, ginger and garlic in a medium saucepan and bring to a boil. Cool in the refrigerator. Combine with the fish in a large bowl, turning to coat evenly. Marinate in the refrigerator for 1 to 4 hours.

2 Drain the fish and season lightly with salt and white pepper. Grill or sear until cooked through or until done to taste. Serve with Wasabi Mashed Potatoes (page 53) and Sweet Sake Bean Sauce (page 53).

Yields 4 servings

nutrition per serving

CAL	CARB	PRO	FAT	FIBER	CHOL	SOD
157	9g	21g	1g	<1g	83mg	720mg

Wasabi Mashed Potatoes

1 Cook the potatoes in enough salted water to cover in a saucepan until tender; drain well. Whip with a mixer or press through a food mill. Add the sour cream, milk, salt and white pepper and beat at low speed until smooth.

2 Add the wasabi gradually, beating constantly and checking frequently for taste; you may not need the entire amount. Add the basil oil for color, if desired.

Yields 6 servings

6 Yukon Gold potatoes, peeled and
   cut into quarters

2 tablespoons nonfat sour cream

1/4 cup 1% milk

salt and white pepper to taste

4 teaspoons (about) prepared wasabi
   (Japanese horseradish)

1 to 2 tablespoons basil oil (optional)

nutrition per serving						
CAL	CARB	PRO	FAT	FIBER	CHOL	SOD
108	27g	5g	<1g	3g	<1mg	24mg

Sweet Sake Black Bean Sauce

1 Combine the beans with enough water to cover in a bowl. Let soak for 1 hour. Sauté the ginger, shallot and garlic in the oil in a saucepan for 3 or 4 minutes or until tender. Add the sake and mirin and cook until reduced by half. Add the chicken stock and cook until reduced by half. Stir in the coconut milk and bring to a boil.

2 Blend the cornstarch with enough water to make a slurry in a bowl. Stir into the boiling mixture and cook until it coats the back of the spoon, stirring constantly.

3 Drain the beans and pat dry. Add the beans to the sauce and season with the sambal, salt and white pepper. Remove to a serving dish and garnish with the papaya. Do not place the papaya in the sauce, as it will break down the thickening agent.

Yields 9 servings

3 tablespoons Chinese black beans

1 tablespoon chopped fresh ginger

1 tablespoon chopped shallot

1 tablespoon chopped garlic

1 tablespoon vegetable oil

1 cup sake

1/2 cup mirin (sweet rice wine)

3/4 cup chicken stock or fish stock

1/4 cup light coconut milk

2 tablespoons cornstarch

1/2 teaspoons sambal (chili sauce)

salt and white pepper to taste

1/4 cup chopped fresh papaya, for garnish

nutrition per serving						
CAL	CARB	PRO	FAT	FIBER	CHOL	SOD
119	14g	1g	2g	2g	<1mg	66mg

week one wednesday

We change the sauce we serve with this weekly to keep it interesting. All the berries are popular, but how about warm chocolate sauce or a compote of pineapple, coconut, and rum? Yummy!

Petite Cal-a-Vie Cheesecake

Graham Cracker Crust

15 graham crackers

1/4 cup almond oil

1 teaspoon cinnamon

Cheesecake

3 cups part-skim ricotta cheese

1/2 cup nonfat vanilla yogurt or nonfat
   cream cheese

2 eggs

2 egg whites

1 1/4 cups Splenda

grated zest of 1 lemon

1 tablespoon cornstarch

3 tablespoons unbleached flour

1 teaspoon vanilla extract

Warm Berry Compote (page 58)

1 For the crust, spray a 9×13-inch baking dish with nonstick cooking spray. Crush the graham crackers in a food processor. Add the almond oil and cinnamon and pulse until the mixture has the consistency of wet sand. Press firmly over the bottom of the prepared baking dish.

2 For the cheesecake, preheat the oven to 375 degrees. Combine the ricotta cheese, yogurt, eggs and egg whites in a food processor. Add the Splenda, lemon zest, cornstarch, flour and vanilla; process for 1 minute or until smooth. Pour evenly over the crust and tap the dish gently on the countertop to remove air bubbles.

3 Place in a large baking pan half filled with hot water. Bake for 45 to 55 minutes or until a knife inserted into the center comes out clean. Cool on a wire rack for 1 hour, then chill for 2 hours or longer. Serve with the Warm Berry Compote.

Yields 20 servings

nutrition per serving						
CAL	CARB	PRO	FAT	FIBER	CHOL	SOD
125	10g	6g	7g	<1g	33mg	94mg

beauty treatments

Cal-a-Vie's advanced Beauty Program was developed in coordination with international health and beauty experts. Beauty and skin care treatments for men and women help to cleanse and invigorate your body. Soothing massage, natural plant and sea extracts, and aromatic restorative oils are an integral component of each of our beauty treatments.

Facials

We utilize only products with a natural affinity for the skin, such as land and sea extracts, essences of flowers and herbs, and healing clays. These soothing treatments purify, hydrate, and revitalize facial tissue.

Hair and Scalp

Deeply relaxing and restorative, the treatments consist of a thorough cleansing, conditioning, and massage to nourish the scalp and reestablish the hair's initial structure. Using plant-based products from Phytologie, this treatment increases blood flow to the scalp, stimulates hair follicles, and normalizes both dry and oily scalps.

Contouring Massage & Cellulite Reduction Treatment

This invigorating massage specifically targets the areas of the hip, stomach, thighs, and buttocks. Concentrated marine actives and serums remove toxins and mobilize fluids that will improve the appearance of the skin, giving it suppleness and a healthy glow.

Ayruvedic Mud Scrub

Using selected herbs and minerals noted for their unique beneficial qualities, our mud scrub will purify, cleanse, and stimulate your body. The vigorous scrub will exfoliate your skin to reveal a polished glow.

Vichy Shower with Body Buffing

Rejuvenate your skin with a customized exfoliating scrub to accelerate skin renewal, lift away surface dryness, and improve skin hydration. Your body will then luxuriate in the cascading waters of our Vichy Shower as all remaining tension is washed away.

Airbrush Tanning

Uplift your spirit with our water-based airbrush tanning system, Totally Tan. Totally Tan is odorless, longer lasting, not drying to the skin, and doesn't contain heavy oils or additives. It is the healthy way to tan without the harmful effects from the sun or tanning booths.

thursday menu
jeudi

breakfast

Ricotta-Stuffed Crepes with
Warm Berry Compote

lunch

Cal-a-Vie Waldorf Fruit Salad
Oven-Roasted Alaskan Halibut

hors d'oeuvre

Gorgonzola Cheese Gougères

dinner

Garden Vegetable Soup
Macadamia-Crusted Apple-Stuffed Duck Breast
with Sweet-and-Sour Red Cabbage

dessert

Maple Vanilla Bean Flan

Ricotta-Stuffed Crepes with Warm Berry Compote

1 Combine the milk, flour mixture, egg, Splenda, almond oil, vanilla and nutmeg in a blender and process at high speed for 30 seconds. Add additional flour or milk, if necessary, for a batter that is thinner than pancake batter but thicker than a malt.

2 Spray a small nonstick crepe pan with nonstick cooking spray and heat over low to medium heat. Ladle in about 1 ounce of batter at a time, or enough to just cover the bottom of the pan, tilting the pan to cover evenly. Cook for 15 to 30 seconds, or until the edge of the batter is light brown. Turn the crepe and cook for 15 to 30 seconds longer or until light brown. Remove to a plate and cool for 10 minutes. Repeat with the remaining batter. You can fill the crepes immediately, let stand at room temperature for up to 4 hours or store in the refrigerator for up to 3 days.

3 Place the crepes on a work surface and spoon the filling onto the crepes. Roll the crepes to enclose the filling and place on serving plates. Spoon 2 tablespoons of the Warm Berry Compote over each serving and garnish with fresh berries.

Yields 10 servings

3/4 cup 1% milk

1/2 cup mixed whole wheat pastry flour and
   unbleached flour

1 egg

2 tablespoons Splenda

1 teaspoon almond oil

1 teaspoon vanilla extract

1/4 teaspoon nutmeg

Ricotta Filling

Warm Berry Compote (page 58)

fresh berries, for garnish

nutrition per serving						
CAL	CARB	PRO	FAT	FIBER	CHOL	SOD
37	6g	2g	1g	<1g	1mg	14mg

Ricotta Filling

Combine the ricotta cheese, cottage cheese, Splenda and cinnamon in a bowl and mix well. Store in the refrigerator until needed.

Yields 6 servings

1 cup part-skim ricotta cheese

1/2 cup nonfat cottage cheese

1/4 cup Splenda or sugar

1 teaspoon cinnamon

nutrition per serving						
CAL	CARB	PRO	FAT	FIBER	CHOL	SOD
74	4g	7g	3g	<1g	14mg	122mg

Warm Berry Compote

1 cup frozen raspberries, thawed

1 cup frozen blueberries, thawed

1³/4 cups orange juice

³/4 cup Splenda

1 tablespoon cornstarch

1 Combine the raspberries, blueberries, orange juice and Splenda in a medium saucepan. Bring to a boil and reduce the heat. Simmer for several minutes, stirring occasionally.

2 Blend the cornstarch with enough water to make a thick slurry in a bowl. Return the berry mixture to a boil and stir in the cornstarch slurry. Cook until the mixture is thick enough to coat the back of the spoon, stirring constantly.

3 Spoon into a blender and process for 30 seconds. Strain through a fine mesh strainer into a bowl and add fresh berries. Let stand for 10 minutes before serving.

Yields 25 servings

nutrition per serving						
CAL	CARB	PRO	FAT	FIBER	CHOL	SOD
19	4g	<1g	<1g	<1g	0mg	<1mg

Cal-a-Vie Waldorf Fruit Salad

1¹/2 Fuji apples

¹/2 pear

1 cup seedless red grapes

¹/4 cup chopped celery

¹/4 cup raisins

2 tablespoons chopped yellow onion, cooked and cooled

2 tablespoons chopped toasted walnuts

¹/2 recipe Mango Mousse (page 33)

1 Cut the apples and pear into bite-size pieces and combine with the grapes, celery and raisins in a medium bowl. Add the onion and walnuts and mix gently. Fold in the Mango Mousse; do not overmix.

2 Chill for 1 hour or up to 3 days. Spoon into chilled cups or serving bowls.

Yields 5 servings

nutrition per serving						
CAL	CARB	PRO	FAT	FIBER	CHOL	SOD
134	28g	2g	3g	3g	0mg	11mg

Alaskan halibut is usually available fresh from March through September or October and frozen year-round. Fresh fava beans are sometimes not available, but you can substitute canned or frozen. To roast the corn, remove the husks and silks and place in a 400-degree oven for 30 to 40 minutes, turning frequently. Cut the kernels from the cooled corn cobs with a sharp knife.

Oven-Roasted Alaskan Halibut

Succotash

kernels from 3 ears of roasted corn

1 cup cooked cannellini or white beans

1 cup cooked fava beans

1 tablespoon extra-virgin olive oil

1 shallot, finely chopped

1 bunch parsley, chopped

Asparagus Sauce

1 bunch large white asparagus

1/4 yellow onion, chopped

2 tablespoons all-purpose flour

3/4 cup chicken stock or fish stock

1/4 cup light coconut milk

salt and pepper to taste

Halibut

1 tablespoon extra-virgin olive oil

4 (4-ounce) fresh or thawed frozen Alaskan
   halibut fillets

salt and pepper to taste

2 sprigs fresh thyme

1 teaspoon crushed garlic

juice of 1/2 lemon

1   For the succotash, mix the corn, cannellini and fava beans in a small bowl. Heat the olive oil in a nonstick sauté pan and add the bean mixture. Sauté for 2 to 3 minutes. Add the shallot and parsley; keep warm.

2   For the sauce, cut off and reserve 1-inch tips from the asparagus spears; cut the stems diagonally into thin slices. Combine the asparagus stems, onion, flour and stock in a saucepan and mix well. Bring to a boil, stirring constantly, and reduce heat. Simmer for 5 to 10 minutes or until the asparagus is tender. Stir in the coconut milk.

3   Process the mixture in a blender or food processor at high speed for 30 seconds. Strain into a saucepan and season with salt and pepper; keep warm. Blanch the reserved asparagus tips in water in a small saucepan.

4   For the halibut, preheat the oven to 450 degrees. Heat the olive oil to smoking in an ovenproof medium sauté pan. Season the fish fillets with salt and pepper. Add to the sauté pan and sear on 1 side until golden brown. Turn the fillets over and add the thyme.

5   Place in the oven and bake for 3 to 4 minutes or just until firm but not dry. Remove from the oven and add the garlic and lemon juice to the pan, swirling to prevent the garlic from browning.

6   To assemble, spoon the succotash into the centers of 4 serving plates. Spoon 2 tablespoons of the asparagus sauce around the succotash. Invert the fish and place seared side up on the succotash; arrange the blanched asparagus tips symmetrically around the fish. Serve immediately.

Yields 4 servings

nutrition per serving

CAL	CARB	PRO	FAT	FIBER	CHOL	SOD
430	38g	42g	13g	10g	47mg	392mg

Gorgonzola Cheese Gougères

3 tablespoons butter

3/4 cup water

3/4 cup unbleached flour

1 egg

3 egg whites

1/2 cup loosely packed crumbled
gorgonzola cheese

1   Preheat the oven to 425 degrees. Melt the butter with the water in a saucepan over low heat. Bring to a boil and add the flour all at once, stirring until the mixture forms a dough. Remove from the heat and let cool.

2   Beat in the egg and egg whites 1 at a time. Fold in the cheese. Spoon into a pastry tube and pipe into 1-inch mounds on a parchment-lined baking sheet. Bake for 5 to 10 minutes or until puffed but not yet beginning to brown. Reduce the temperature to 350 degrees and bake for 10 minutes longer or until crisp and golden brown.

Yields 40 gougères

nutrition per gougère

CAL	CARB	PRO	FAT	FIBER	CHOL	SOD
25	2g	1g	2g	1g	9mg	38mg

Garden Vegetable Soup

1 Heat the olive oil in a saucepan and add the cauliflower, onion and celery. Sauté for 2 minutes. Add the wine and cook for several minutes to evaporate the alcohol. Stir in the stock and bring to a boil. Reduce the temperature and simmer for 20 minutes or until the vegetables are tender.

2 Process the soup in a blender until smooth and season with salt and pepper. Spoon into soup bowls and garnish with nutmeg and fresh dill weed.

Yields 6 servings

1 teaspoon olive oil

1 head cauliflower, chopped

1 onion, chopped

2 ribs celery, chopped

1/4 cup white wine

4 cups vegetable stock or roasted
   chicken stock

salt and pepper to taste

1 teaspoon nutmeg, for garnish

6 sprigs fresh dill weed, for garnish

61

nutrition per serving						
CAL	CARB	PRO	FAT	FIBER	CHOL	SOD
62	9g	3g	2g	3g	1mg	505mg

Macadamia-Crusted Apple-Stuffed Duck Breast with Sweet-and-Sour Red Cabbage

Sweet-and-Sour Red Cabbage

1 small red onion, minced

1 teaspoon vegetable oil or butter

2 tablespoons all-purpose flour

1/2 cup chicken stock

1 Granny Smith apple, minced

1 head red cabbage, thinly sliced

1/2 cup raspberry vinaigrette

1/2 cup red wine

salt and pepper to taste

Macadamia Crust

2 ounces toasted macadamia nuts

3/4 cup panko (Japanese bread crumbs)

1/4 cup chopped fresh cilantro

1 teaspoon sugar or Splenda

1/2 teaspoon curry powder

1 teaspoon butter or vegetable oil

Duck

2 tablespoons minced red onion

1 teaspoon butter

3 Fuji apples, chopped

2 tablespoons dried cranberries or dried cherries

2 tablespoons Calvados

1 cinnamon stick

4 boneless skinless duck breasts

salt and pepper to taste

Dijon mustard

1   For the cabbage, sauté the onion in the oil in a saucepan until translucent. Add the flour and cook for 2 minutes, stirring constantly. Add the stock, apple, cabbage, raspberry vinaigrette, wine, salt and pepper; mix well. Simmer for 20 to 30 minutes or until the cabbage is tender. Keep warm.

2   For the macadamia crust, combine the macadamia nuts, panko, cilantro, sugar, curry powder and butter in a food processor. Process until the consistency of cornmeal.

3   For the duck, preheat the oven to 500 degrees. Sauté the onion in the butter in a saucepan until tender. Add the apples, cranberries, Calvados and cinnamon stick. Simmer for 5 minutes. Cool and remove and discard the cinnamon stick.

4   Season each duck breast on both sides with salt and pepper. Cut a pocket in each duck breast. Spoon the apple filling into the duck and secure the opening with skewers. Sear the duck on both sides in a nonstick skillet. Brush with Dijon mustard and coat with the macadamia crust. Place on a baking sheet and roast for 8 to 12 minutes or until cooked through. Serve with the sweet-and-sour red cabbage.

Yields 4 servings

nutrition per serving

CAL	CARB	PRO	FAT	FIBER	CHOL	SOD
571	64g	30g	19g	12g	90mg	370mg

Maple Vanilla Bean Flan

1 For the flan, scald the milk in a saucepan and add the maple syrup. Scrape the seeds from the vanilla bean and add both the seeds and the bean to the milk mixture. Let stand for 25 minutes.

2 Beat the eggs with the egg whites in a bowl and add to the cooled milk with the nutmeg and cinnamon, blending well. Strain and remove the froth and vanilla bean.

3 Preheat the oven to 325 degrees. Spoon into custard cups and place in a water bath in a baking pan. Bake for $1^1/2$ hours or until a knife inserted into the center comes out clean.

4 For the topping, combine the red apple, green apple, apple juice, brown sugar and cinnamon in a saucepan. Cook just until the apples are tender; do not overcook.

5 Invert the flans onto serving plates and top with the sauce. Garnish each serving with a mint sprig and a raspberry.

Yields 12 servings

Flan

4 cups 1% milk

1 cup pure maple syrup

1 vanilla bean, split lengthwise, or
   $1^1/2$ teaspoons vanilla extract

4 eggs

3 egg whites

$1/2$ teaspoon nutmeg

$1/2$ teaspoon ground cinnamon

Apple Topping

1 red apple, minced

1 green apple, minced

$1/4$ cup apple juice

1 tablespoon brown sugar

$1/2$ teaspoon ground cinnamon

12 mint sprigs, for garnish

12 raspberries, for garnish

nutrition per serving						
CAL	CARB	PRO	FAT	FIBER	CHOL	SOD
156	28g	6g	3g	1g	76mg	81mg

friday menu

breakfast

Broiled Grapefruit

Banana Nut Muffins

Poached Egg

lunch

Cal-a-Vie Turkey Cheeseburger

with Chipotle Mayonnaise on Homemade Sun-Dried Tomato Buns

Minted Iced Oranges

hors d'oeuvre

Blue Crab Nori Rolls

dinner

Firecracker Spinach Salad with Orange Sesame Dressing

Sweet Soy-Glazed Swordfish

with Chinese Long Beans and Mango Cilantro Rice

dessert

Silken Chocolate Mousse

We serve Banana Nut Muffins with broiled ruby red grapefruit and poached eggs. We cut the grapefruit into halves, cut around the sections, sprinkle them with brown sugar and cinnamon and broil until golden brown.

Banana Nut Muffins

1 Preheat the oven to 350 degrees. Beat the honey and almond oil with a wooden spoon in a bowl until very smooth. Beat in the eggs 1 at a time, and then mix in the bananas. Sift in the flour, baking powder and salt and mix well. Fold in the walnuts.

2 Spoon into 18 muffin cups sprayed with nonstick cooking spray. Bake for 25 minutes or until the muffins test done. You may also bake in a 5x9-inch loaf pan for 1 hour if preferred.

Yields 18 servings

1/3 **cup honey**

1/4 **cup almond oil or softened butter**

2 **eggs, or 4 egg whites**

2 **cups mashed very ripe bananas**

2 **cups whole wheat pastry flour**

3/4 **teaspoon baking powder**

1/2 **teaspoon salt**

2/3 **cup chopped walnuts**

nutrition per serving

CAL	CARB	PRO	FAT	FIBER	CHOL	SOD
142	20g	3g	6g	2g	22mg	100mg

week one friday

We would not think of removing this lunch from our repertoire! After a decade, we have only made it better with homemade low-fat chipotle mayonnaise and sliced mozzarella.

Cal-a-Vie Turkey Cheeseburgers with Chipotle Mayonnaise

66

1 pound ground turkey

1 tablespoon chopped shallot

1 tablespoon chopped scallions

1 teaspoon chopped garlic

1 egg, or 2 egg whites

2 teaspoons Worcestershire sauce

1 tablespoon chopped fresh tarragon

1 teaspoon salt

1/2 teaspoon pepper

wheat germ (optional)

2 tablespoons Chipotle Mayonnaise
    (page 67)

4 Homemade Sun-Dried Tomato Buns
    (page 67)

4 slices mozzarella cheese

lettuce, tomato, onion and pickle,
    for garnish

1 Combine the ground turkey, shallot, scallions, garlic, egg, Worcestershire sauce, tarragon, salt and pepper in a bowl and mix well. Add wheat germ if needed to bind the mixture. Shape into 4 patties. Grill the patties until cooked through.

2 Spread the Chipotle Mayonnaise on the Homemade Sun-Dried Tomato Buns and add 1 turkey patty and 1 slice of cheese to each burger. Garnish with lettuce, tomato, onion and pickle.

Yields 4 servings

nutrition per serving						
CAL	CARB	PRO	FAT	FIBER	CHOL	SOD
192	2g	21g	10g	<1g	136mg	732mg

Whole Wheat Sun-Dried Tomato Buns

1 Dissolve the yeast in a mixture of 2 cups water and the honey in a bowl; let stand until frothy to activate the yeast. Add the sun-dried tomatoes, oil, whole wheat flour, unbleached flour, garlic powder and salt; mix with a mixer or by hand. Knead on a floured surface for 5 minutes or until smooth and elastic.

2 Place in an oiled bowl, turning to coat the surface. Let rise, covered, in a warm place until doubled in bulk. Divide into 10 portions and shape into balls. Flatten into buns and place on a baking sheet lightly sprayed with nonstick cooking spray. Sprinkle with cornmeal, brush with the egg white mixture and sprinkle with the sesame seeds.

3 Preheat the oven to 400 degrees. Bake the buns for 25 minutes or until golden brown. Remove to a wire rack and cool for 5 minutes before slicing to fill.

Yields 10 buns

2 tablespoons dry yeast

2 cups warm water

1 tablespoon honey or sugar

8 sun-dried tomatoes, chopped

2 teaspoons vegetable oil

2 cups whole wheat pastry flour

2 cups unbleached flour

1 teaspoon garlic powder

1 teaspoon salt

2 tablespoons cornmeal

1 egg white, beaten with
    2 teaspoons water

2 tablespoons sesame seeds

nutrition per serving

CAL	CARB	PRO	FAT	FIBER	CHOL	SOD
104	19g	3g	2g	3g	0mg	38mg

Chipotle Mayonnaise

Combine the chipotle chile, tofu, mayonnaise, ketchup and Dijon mustard in a food processor and process until smooth.

Yields 16 (2-tablespoon) servings

1 chipotle chile

3 ounces silken tofu

3 tablespoons nonfat mayonnaise

3 tablespoons ketchup

2 teaspoons Dijon mustard

nutrition per serving

CAL	CARB	PRO	FAT	FIBER	CHOL	SOD
12	2g	1g	<1g	<1g	<1mg	76mg

Minted Iced Oranges

14 (or more) oranges

8 mint sprigs

2/3 cup sugar

1/2 cup water

juice of 1 lemon

8 fresh bay leaves or citrus leaves,
    for garnish

nutrition per serving						
CAL	CARB	PRO	FAT	FIBER	CHOL	SOD
90	28g	1g	<1g	1g	0mg	2mg

1 Slice off the tops of 8 of the oranges, reserving the tops. Scoop out and reserve the flesh. Freeze the orange shells and tops.

2 Combine the mint sprigs, sugar, water and half the lemon juice in a heavy saucepan and mix well. Cook over low heat until the sugar dissolves. Bring to a boil and boil for 2 to 3 minutes or until the syrup is clear; remove and discard the mint.

3 Grate the zest from the remaining 6 oranges and add to the syrup. Squeeze enough juice from the scooped out orange flesh and the grated oranges, using additional oranges if necessary, to measure 3 cups juice. Stir the orange juice and the remaining lemon juice into the syrup. Adjust the amount of lemon juice and sugar to taste.

4 Pour the mixture into a shallow dish and freeze for 3 hours. Remove to a mixing bowl and whisk to break up ice crystals. Freeze for 3 to 4 hour longer or until firm but not solid.

5 Spoon the frozen mixture into the frozen orange shells, mounding it over the rim; top with the frozen top slices. Return to the freezer until serving time. Pierce a small hole in each top slice and place a bay leaf in the hole.

Yields 8 servings

To make green onion florettes, wash and trim the roots and green tops from green onions, leaving 4-inch stems. Slice the onion stems in narrow lengthwise strips, starting about 2 inches from the bulb and cutting through all the layers to the end. Place in ice water until the strips curl.

Blue Crab Nori Rolls

1 Bring the water to a boil in a saucepan and add the rice. Reduce the heat and simmer for 20 to 30 minutes or until tender but still firm. Remove to a bowl and add the vinegar and mirin, fluffing with a wooden spoon; cool completely.

2 Arrange a sushi mat on a work surface and place 1 sheet of nori at a time on the mat. Place 1/4 cup of the rice on the nori. Spread a small amount of plum paste on the bottom 1/4 of the sheet, then add a small amount of wasabi and a strip of carrot, a strip of cucumber, a strip of avocado and a strip of green onion. Top with blue crab meat.

3 Roll the nori with the help of the sushi mat. Cut the roll into 1-inch pieces. Repeat the process to use all the nori sheets.

4 Serve with the soy sauce and additional wasabi. Garnish with sunflower greens, shredded red cabbage, shredded daikon, preserved ginger and green onion florets.

Yields 24 (2-roll) servings

2 cups water

1 cup uncooked sushi rice

1 tablespoon rice vinegar

1 tablespoon mirin (sweet rice wine)

6 sheets nori (seaweed)

3 tablespoons plum paste

2 tablespoons wasabi
    (Japanese horseradish)

1/2 carrot, peeled and cut into thin strips

1/2 cucumber, cut into thin strips

1/2 avocado, thinly sliced

5 green onions, cut into strips

8 ounces blue crab meat, drained

2 tablespoons low-sodium soy sauce or
    Bragg's Liquid Aminos

1 tablespoon wasabi

sunflower greens, shredded red cabbage,
    shredded daikon, preserved ginger and
    green onion florets, for garnish

week one friday

nutrition per serving						
CAL	CARB	PRO	FAT	FIBER	CHOL	SOD
58	10g	3g	1g	<1g	7mg	55mg

This salad was inspired by Chef Dave Armour in 1989 and can be prepared with any lettuce. We like to add hoisin-crusted shrimp to this, just warm enough to wilt the spinach, and, of course, some homemade bread hot out of the oven.

Firecracker Spinach Salad with Orange Sesame Dressing

Orange Sesame Dressing

1 cup orange juice

1 teaspoon honey

2 teaspoons sesame oil

1 tablespoon soy sauce

2 tablespoons rice wine vinegar

1/4 cup water

1 teaspoon hot red pepper sauce (optional)

1 shallot, chopped

2 teaspoons grated fresh ginger

Salad

6 cups washed baby spinach

1/4 cup daikon sprouts

1/4 cup julienned carrot

1/4 cup julienned jicama

2 tablespoons mixture of black sesame
seeds and white sesame seeds,
for garnish

1   For the dressing, cook the orange juice in a saucepan until reduced by half. Combine with the honey, sesame oil, soy sauce, vinegar, water and hot sauce in a blender. Add the shallot and ginger and process until smooth. Store in the refrigerator.

2   For the salad, mix the spinach, daikon sprouts, carrot and jicama in large bowl. Add the dressing and toss to coat well. Garnish with the sesame seeds.

Yields 4 servings

nutrition per serving						
CAL	CARB	PRO	FAT	FIBER	CHOL	SOD
111	14g	4g	5g	2g	0mg	298mg

This recipe is a Cal-a-Vie Friday night cooking class favorite. The swordfish should be firm and white with no fat and no blood line. Try to find fillets at least ¼- to ½-inch thick and take care to cook the swordfish all the way through.

Sweet Soy-Glazed Swordfish with Chinese Long Beans and Mango Cilantro Rice

1 tablespoon mirin (sweet rice wine)

1 tablespoon light soy sauce or Bragg's Liquid Aminos

½ teaspoon sambal (chili sauce)

1 tablespoon chopped shallot

2 teaspoons chopped fresh ginger

4 (3-ounce) swordfish fillets

Mango Cilantro Rice (page 73)

12 Chinese long beans, steamed

Maple Soy Reduction (page 22)

orchids and cilantro sprigs, for garnish

1 Combine the mirin, soy sauce, sambal, shallot and ginger in a bowl and mix well. Add the fish, coating evenly. Marinate in the refrigerator for 20 minutes.

2 Drain the fillets and discard the marinade. Grill for several minutes on each side or until cooked through.

3 Spoon the Mango Cilantro Rice onto serving plates. Wrap the long beans around the fish fillets and place on the rice. Drizzle with Maple Soy Reduction and garnish with an orchid and a sprig of cilantro.

4 Nutritional analysis includes the Mango Cilantro Rice. It does not include the Maple Soy Reduction.

Yields 4 servings

nutrition per serving

CAL	CARB	PRO	FAT	FIBER	CHOL	SOD
440	75g	22g	7g	8g	9mg	320mg

Mango Cilantro Rice

1 Simmer the rice in the stock and coconut milk in a saucepan until the rice is tender and the liquid is absorbed.

2 Sauté the mango, cilantro and bell pepper in a nonstick sauté pan for several minutes. Add to the rice and mix well. Keep warm.

Yields 4 servings

1 cup uncooked brown rice

1 1/2 cups vegetable stock or chicken stock

1/2 cup light coconut milk

1 mango, chopped

2 tablespoons chopped cilantro

1/4 cup chopped red bell pepper

nutrition per serving

CAL	CARB	PRO	FAT	FIBER	CHOL	SOD
237	47g	4g	4g	3g	0mg	107mg

Silken Chocolate Mousse

1 Combine the tofu, baking cocoa, maple syrup, Kahlúa, vanilla and cinnamon in a food processor fitted with a metal blade. Process for 7 to 10 minutes or until very smooth and thick.

2 Chill for 20 minutes. Spoon into dessert cups and garnish with raspberries and mint.

Yields 6 servings

2 (12-ounce) packages Mori-Nu lite
    extra-firm silken tofu

1/2 cup baking cocoa

1/2 cup pure maple syrup

2 tablespoons Kahlúa

1 tablespoon vanilla extract

1 teaspoon ground cinnamon

raspberries and mint sprigs, for garnish

nutrition per serving

CAL	CARB	PRO	FAT	FIBER	CHOL	SOD
149	26g	9g	2g	2g	0mg	104mg

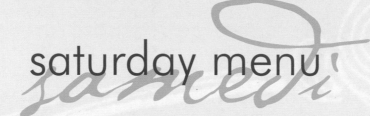

breakfast

Homemade Granola with Warm Apple Compote

lunch

Asian Chicken Salad with Spicy Hoisin Dressing

Protein Pickup Smoothie

hors d'oeuvre

Broiled Tomato Crostini

dinner

Barley Vegetable Soup

Roasted Tenderloin of Beef with Cabernet Sauce

Lobster Mashed Potatoes

dessert

Chocolate Seashells

Homemade Granola

1 Preheat the oven to 325 degrees. Mix the oats, sunflower seeds and almonds in a bowl. Combine the bananas, maple syrup, almond oil and cinnamon in a bowl and mix until smooth. Add 2/3 of the banana mixture to the oat mixture and mix well.

2 Spread the mixture on a baking sheet with sides sprayed with butter-flavor nonstick cooking spray. Bake for 25 minutes, stirring every 10 to 15 minutes.

3 Add the cereal, wheat germ and salt to the remaining banana mixture. Add to the baked oat mixture and mix well. Turn off the oven and place the granola in the oven. Let stand until cool. You can add cranberries or other dried fruit after the mixture cools, if desired.

Yields 20 (1-ounce) servings

4 cups rolled oats

1/3 cup unsalted sunflower seeds

1/3 cup sliced almonds

2 ripe bananas, mashed

1/2 cup pure maple syrup

2 tablespoons almond oil

2 teaspoons ground cinnamon

3 cups honey puffed Kashi cereal

3/4 cup toasted wheat germ

1/4 teaspoon salt

nutrition per serving

CAL	CARB	PRO	FAT	FIBER	CHOL	SOD
96	15g	3g	3g	2g	0mg	2mg

Warm Apple Compote

1 Chop the apricots and soak in 1 cup water in a saucepan for 1 hour. Bring to a simmer and simmer over low heat for 15 minutes. Add the apples, raisins, lemon juice and cinnamon and mix well. Simmer for 15 to 20 minutes longer or until the apples are tender, stirring occasionally.

2 Preheat the oven to 350 degrees. Spoon the apple mixture into a 1-quart baking dish or 6 individual ramekins. Top with granola and bake for 10 minutes. Serve with a dollop of vanilla yogurt.

Yields 6 servings

2/3 cup dried unsulphured apricots

3 tart apples, peeled and sliced

2 tablespoons raisins or dried currants

2 teaspoons lemon juice

1/2 teaspoon ground cinnamon or ground allspice

2/3 cup Homemade Granola (above)

3/4 cup nonfat or low-fat vanilla yogurt

nutrition per serving

CAL	CARB	PRO	FAT	FIBER	CHOL	SOD
162	34g	4g	3g	5g	1mg	23mg

week one saturday

This popular salad can be served for lunch or dinner. You can substitute shrimp, turkey or tofu for the chicken. Be sure to add the dressing at the last minute to ensure crispness.

Asian Chicken Salad with Spicy Hoisin Dressing

2 egg roll wrappers

1¹/4 cups sliced almonds

8 cups mixed baby greens

4 ounces bean sprouts

1 cup julienned carrots

3 cups julienned napa cabbage

¹/4 red onion, julienned

6 (4¹/2-ounce) boneless
   chicken breasts, trimmed

salt and pepper to taste

³/4 cup Spicy Hoisin Dressing (page 77)

bean sprouts and black sesame seeds,
   for garnish

1   Preheat the oven to 450 degrees. Arrange the egg roll wrappers on a nonstick baking sheet sprayed lightly with nonstick cooking spray. Bake just until golden brown. Remove from the oven and cut immediately into ¹/2-inch strips.

2   Reduce the oven temperature to 350 degrees. Spread the almonds on a baking sheet and toast until golden brown. Combine the egg roll wrapper strips and toasted almonds with the baby greens, bean sprouts, carrots, cabbage and onion in a large bowl. Place in the refrigerator until ready to serve.

3   Season the chicken with salt and pepper. Grill or sauté to an internal temperature of 160 to 165 degrees. Cool at room temperature for about 5 minutes and cut each breast into 3 lengthwise strips.

4   Add the Spicy Hoisin Dressing to the salad and toss to coat well. Spoon the salad onto serving plates and top each serving with 3 slices of chicken. Garnish with additional bean sprouts and black sesame seeds.

5   Nutritional analysis includes the salad and dressing.

Yields 6 servings

nutrition per serving

CAL	CARB	PRO	FAT	FIBER	CHOL	SOD
442	31g	37g	15g	9g	70mg	1609mg

Spicy Hoisin Dressing

1 Combine the hoisin sauce, mirin, rice vinegar, soy sauce, sesame oil, vegetable oil, sambal, garlic, shallot, ginger, salt and pepper with the water in a blender. Process at high speed for 1 minute.

2 Add the xanthan gum gradually, processing constantly until the mixture thickens. Store in the refrigerator.

Yields 6 servings

2 tablespoons hoisin sauce

1/2 cup mirin (sweet rice wine)

1/2 cup unseasoned rice vinegar

1/4 cup light soy sauce

1 teaspoon sesame oil

1 teaspoon vegetable oil

1 teaspoon sambal (chili sauce)

2 garlic cloves

1 large shallot

1 tablespoon chopped fresh ginger

salt and pepper to taste

1 cup cold filtered water

1 teaspoon xanthan gum

nutrition per serving							
CAL	CARB	PRO	FAT	FIBER	CHOL	SOD	
73	9g	0g	2g	0g	0mg	685mg	

Protein Pickup Smoothie

8 ounces frozen blueberries

2 strawberries

1 cup chopped fresh pineapple

1 cup orange juice

1 teaspoon flax seed oil

1 scoop vanilla protein powder

2 tablespoons Splenda

1 Combine the blueberries, strawberries, pineapple, orange juice, flax seed oil, protein powder and Splenda in a blender and process at high speed for 1 minute. Add additional orange juice if the mixture is too thick and additional blueberries if it is too thin.

2 Pour into chilled glasses and garnish with a strawberry half and a pineapple wedge.

Yields 6 (^{1}/2-cup) servings

nutrition per serving

CAL	CARB	PRO	FAT	FIBER	CHOL	SOD
64	13g	2g	1g	2g	3mg	4mg

Broiled Tomato Crostini

2 large red tomatoes, peeled, seeded
  and chopped

1 yellow tomato, peeled, seeded
  and chopped

2 garlic cloves, minced

2 tablespoons olive oil

1 teaspoon balsamic vinegar

1 tablespoon chopped fresh basil

salt and pepper to taste

1 baguette

grated Parmesan cheese and fresh basil,
  for garnish

1 Combine the tomatoes, garlic, olive oil, vinegar, basil, salt and pepper in a bowl. Marinate for 1 hour.

2 Preheat the broiler. Slice the baguette into thin slices and arrange the slices on a baking sheet. Toast until light brown on both sides. Spread the tomato mixture on the toasted rounds and return to the baking sheet. Broil for 3 to 4 minutes longer. Garnish with Parmesan cheese and additional basil; serve immediately.

Yields 7 servings

nutrition per serving

CAL	CARB	PRO	FAT	FIBER	CHOL	SOD
75	7g	1g	5g	1g	0mg	64mg

Barley Vegetable Soup

¹/4 cup dried lentils

1¹/2 cups uncooked barley

5 cups chicken stock or vegetable stock

1 tablespoon olive oil

2 garlic cloves, minced

1 leek bulb, cut into ¹/2-inch pieces
(about 1¹/2 cups)

12 cups defatted chicken broth

5 carrots, chopped

2 ribs celery, chopped

2 cups broccoli florets

1 red bell pepper, cut into ¹/2-inch pieces

1 jalapeño chile, seeded and minced
(optional)

1 tablespoon oregano

1 tablespoon basil

1 teaspoon thyme

1 bay leaf

cayenne pepper to taste

¹/2 teaspoon black pepper

3 cups Revitalizer (page 159) or
tomato juice

2 tablespoons miso (bean paste)

3 tablespoons water

¹/2 cup minced chives or parsley

basil, for garnish

1 Soak the lentils in water to cover in a bowl. Rinse the barley and combine with the stock in a large saucepan. Cook for about 2 hours or until the barley is tender. Drain the lentils and add to the saucepan. Cook for 30 minutes, adding additional stock, if needed.

2 Heat the olive oil in a large saucepan and add the garlic and leek. Sauté for 3 to 4 minutes or until the leek is tender. Add the chicken broth, carrots, celery, broccoli, bell pepper, jalapeño chile, oregano, basil, thyme, bay leaf, cayenne pepper and black pepper. Stir in the barley, lentils and tomato juice. Simmer for 30 to 40 minutes or until the vegetables are tender.

3 Blend the miso with the water in a cup. Add to the soup and mix well. Cook until heated through; remove and discard the bay leaf. Serve hot and sprinkle with chives. Garnish with additional basil.

Yields 17 servings

nutrition per serving						
CAL	CARB	PRO	FAT	FIBER	CHOL	SOD
125	23g	6g	2g	5g	<1mg	516mg

week one saturday

Roasted Tenderloin of Beef

1 For the sauce, combine the wine with the shallots, parsley and peppercorns in a medium saucepan. Cook until reduced almost to a syrup. Add the demi-glace and cook until the mixture coats the back of the spoon. Season with salt and pepper and strain through a fine strainer into the saucepan. Keep warm.

2 For the beef, preheat the oven to 500 degrees. Season the beef generously with salt and pepper. Sear on all sides in an ovenproof pan on top of the stove. Insert a meat thermometer and roast in the oven to an internal temperature of 125 to 130 degrees for medium rare.

3 Let stand for 5 minutes before slicing into 1/2-inch medallions. Drizzle with the sauce and serve with Lobster Mashed Potatoes (page 81) and asparagus.

Yields 8 servings

Cabernet Sauce

1 cup cabernet

4 shallots, chopped

1/4 cup chopped parsley

1 tablespoon black peppercorns

1 cup veal demi-glace or
    chicken demi-glace

salt and pepper to taste

			nutrition per serving			
CAL	CARB	PRO	FAT	FIBER	CHOL	SOD
42	4g	1g	1g	<1g	<1mg	127mg

Tenderloin

1 (21/2-pound) beef tenderloin, trimmed

salt and pepper to taste

			nutrition per serving			
CAL	CARB	PRO	FAT	FIBER	CHOL	SOD
240	<1g	24g	16g	0g	71mg	73mg

Lobster Mashed Potatoes

2 uncooked medium Maine lobster tails or
  Baja lobster tails
6 Yukon Gold potatoes, peeled
  and chopped
salt to taste
2 tablespoons nonfat sour cream
1/4 cup nonfat milk
white pepper to taste
lobster oil and/or chopped chives (optional)

1   Steam the lobster tails for 8 minutes; drain and set aside to cool. Crush the tails gently to loosen the meat from the shell and remove the meat. Reserve the shells in the freezer for another use. Chop the meat into 1/4-inch pieces.

2   Combine the potatoes with enough salted cold water to cover in a saucepan. Bring to a boil and cook until tender; drain. Combine with the sour cream, milk, salt and white pepper in a mixing bowl. Beat until smooth. Fold in the lobster meat. Add a dash of lobster oil or chives, if desired.

Yields 6 servings

nutrition per serving

CAL	CARB	PRO	FAT	FIBER	CHOL	SOD
155	28g	13g	1g	3g	32mg	173mg

Chocolate Seashells

1   Preheat the oven to 350 degrees. Sift the whole wheat flour, unbleached flour, baking cocoa and baking powder together. Cream the butter and sugar in a mixing bowl until light and fluffy. Beat in the egg whites and Chocolate Fondue. Dissolve the coffee granules in 6 tablespoons apple juice and add to the batter; mix well. Add the flour mixture 1 tablespoon at a time, mixing well after each addition.

2   Spoon about 1 tablespoon of the batter into each Madeleine mold sprayed with nonstick cooking spray, filling about 2/3 full. Bake for 10 to 12 minutes or just until set; do not overbake. Remove from the molds and cool on a wire rack.

3   Combine the strawberries and 1/4 cup apple juice in a saucepan. Simmer until tender and strain. Spoon 1 tablespoon of the strawberry mixture onto each of 18 serving plates. Scoop the frozen yogurt into the strawberry mixture with a large melon ball scoop.

4   Split the madeleines into halves lengthwise and prop the halves against the yogurt. Garnish with edible flowers.

Yields 18 servings

1/4 cup whole wheat pastry flour
1/2 cup unbleached flour
1/4 cup baking cocoa
1 teaspoon baking powder
1 tablespoon unsalted butter, softened
6 tablespoons sugar or fructose
2 egg whites, lightly beaten
2 1/2 ounces Chocolate Fondue (page 44)
1 tablespoon instant coffee granules
6 tablespoons unfiltered apple juice
1 cup strawberries or raspberries
1/4 cup apple juice or strawberry
  guava nectar
2 to 3 cups nonfat vanilla frozen yogurt
edible flowers, for garnish

nutrition per serving

CAL	CARB	PRO	FAT	FIBER	CHOL	SOD
68	14g	2g	1g	1g	2mg	33mg

week one saturday

week two

At Cal-a-Vie, each of our twenty-four guest cottages has been individually decorated to recall the serene luxury of a European country villa, with terra-cotta roofs, wide wooden plank doors, and window boxes brimming with flowers. Luxuriously appointed with fine linens and handcrafted furniture, each villa is uniquely decorated to welcome and relax you.

Every window at Cal-a-Vie frames an appealing vista, and from your private terrace or balcony you can enjoy breathtaking views of the rolling, wooded hills. Many repeat guests marvel at the uniqueness and special flavor that a week in a different villa provides.

Guests can enjoy meals in our comfortable and inviting dining room, as well as in our beautiful and serene courtyards. Relax in one of our handsome rooms, or curl up by the fire with a good book. Even an evening on the veranda with just the stars will make your stay at Cal-a-Vie a comfortable and memorable experience.

Dimanche sunday menu

breakfast

Mario's Baja Omelet

lunch

Grapefruit and Avocado Salad with Crab Claws

Toasted Hazelnut Biscotti

hors d'oeuvre

Crimini Mushrooms Stuffed with Quinoa

Dinner

Mixed Baby Greens with Roasted Tomato Vinaigrette

Herb-Crusted Salmon with Port Reduction

Saffron Risotto

dessert

Apple Spice Cake with Cinnamon Cream

This dish was named for Cal-a-Vie's eleven-year veteran cook Mario Gullien. He cooks the omelets to order every Sunday morning.

Mario's Baja Omelet

1 Spray a nonstick omelet pan with nonstick cooking spray. Place over low to medium heat. Add the zucchini and cook for 3 minutes or until tender. Add the spinach and season with salt and pepper.

2 Beat the egg with the egg whites in a bowl. Pour into the omelet pan and reduce the heat. Tilt the pan to cover the pan evenly and cook until set but not brown. Sprinkle with the cheese and fold the omelet with a rubber spatula. Remove to a serving plate and serve with the salsa and fresh fruit.

Yields 1 serving

$^{1}/_{2}$ **cup chopped zucchini**

$^{1}/_{2}$ **cup baby spinach**

salt and pepper to taste

1 egg

2 egg whites

2 tablespoons shredded part-skim mozzarella cheese

2 tablespoons Mario's Salsa (below)

nutrition per serving						
CAL	CARB	PRO	FAT	FIBER	CHOL	SOD
165	5g	18g	8g	1g	219mg	277mg

1 Combine the tomatoes, avocado, onion, cilantro, jalapeño chile, lime juice, salt and pepper in a bowl and mix well.

2 Store in the refrigerator.

Yields 6 servings

Mario's Salsa

2 Roma tomatoes or other tomatoes, finely chopped

$^{1}/_{4}$ **avocado, finely chopped**

2 tablespoons chopped red onion

1 tablespoon chopped cilantro

$^{1}/_{4}$ **teaspoon minced jalapeño chile**

1 teaspoon lime juice

salt and pepper to taste

nutrition per serving						
CAL	CARB	PRO	FAT	FIBER	CHOL	SOD
11	1g	<1g	1g	<1g	0mg	30mg

week two sunday

Grapefruit and Avocado Salad with Crab Claws

2 or 3 large ruby red grapefruit

1 small avocado

12 cups spring mix

15 ounces Citrus Juice Dressing (below)

12 cooked crab claws

16 cherry tomatoes

8 whole wheat stone-ground
    sesame crackers

1   Peel the grapefruit and separate into sections in a bowl, reserving enough of the juice for the dressing to measure 1 cup. Peel and seed the avocado and cut into 12 slices.

2   Toss the spring mix with the dressing in a bowl. Spoon onto 4 serving plates. Arrange 6 to 8 sections of grapefruit, 3 slices of avocado and 3 crab claws over each serving. Top with the cherry tomatoes and serve with the crackers.

Yields 4 servings

nutrition per serving

CAL	CARB	PRO	FAT	FIBER	CHOL	SOD
369	46g	13g	17g	10g	28mg	197mg

Citrus Juice Dressing

1 cup fresh grapefruit juice

1/2 cup fresh orange juice

2 garlic cloves

2 tablespoons chopped fresh shallots

2 tablespoons almond oil

1/2 tablespoon Dijon mustard

1/8 teaspoon cumin

1/8 teaspoon hot red pepper sauce

Combine the reserved grapefruit juice, orange juice, garlic, shallots, almond oil, Dijon mustard, cumin and hot sauce in a blender and process until smooth.

Yields 15 ounces

nutrition per serving

CAL	CARB	PRO	FAT	FIBER	CHOL	SOD
426	42g	4g	28g	1g	0mg	197mg

Toasted Hazelnut Biscotti

2 cups unbleached flour

2 cups whole wheat pastry flour

2 teaspoons baking powder

1/2 teaspoon salt

1/2 cup chopped toasted hazelnuts

2 tablespoons butter, softened

1/2 cup sugar

1/2 cup honey

2 eggs

2 egg whites

2 teaspoons crushed or ground
   anise seeds

1 teaspoon vanilla extract

2 tablespoons grated orange zest

2 tablespoons grated lemon zest

1 Preheat the oven to 350 degrees. Sift the unbleached flour, whole wheat flour, baking powder and salt together. Mix in the hazelnuts. Cream the butter, sugar and honey in a mixing bowl until light and fluffy. Beat in the eggs and egg whites, anise seeds, vanilla, orange zest and lemon zest. Add the hazelnut mixture and mix well.

2 Shape into 3 long rolls 1 inch in diameter on a greased nonstick baking sheet. Bake for 15 minutes and cool slightly. Cut each log diagonally into 16 slices. Arrange the slices on the baking sheet and bake for 10 minutes. Turn the slices over and bake for 10 minutes longer.

Yields 48 servings

nutrition per serving						
CAL	CARB	PRO	FAT	FIBER	CHOL	SOD
70	13g	2g	2g	1g	12mg	50mg

Cremini Mushrooms Stuffed with Quinoa

1 Bring the stock to a boil in a saucepan. Add the quinoa and reduce the heat. Simmer, covered, for 20 minutes. Remove from the heat and let stand for 10 to 15 minutes; fluff with a fork.

2 Preheat the oven to 375 degrees. Sauté the shallots and garlic in a medium saucepan sprayed with nonstick cooking spray for several minutes. Add the quinoa, pine nuts, basil, parsley, cheese, salt and pepper and mix well.

3 Spoon the mixture into the mushroom caps and arrange in a baking pan. Add the wine and bake for 20 minutes. Garnish with parsley or basil leaves.

Yields 12 servings

2 cups vegetable stock

1 cup uncooked quinoa

3 tablespoons chopped shallots

3 garlic cloves, chopped

1/2 cup toasted pine nuts

2 tablespoons chopped fresh basil

3 tablespoons chopped Italian parsley

1/4 cup grated Parmesan cheese

salt and pepper to taste

24 cremini mushroom caps

1/2 cup white wine

parsley or basil leaves, for garnish

nutrition per serving						
CAL	CARB	PRO	FAT	FIBER	CHOL	SOD
119	13g	5g	5g	2g	1mg	77mg

Mixed Baby Greens with Roasted Tomato Vinaigrette

1 Preheat the oven to 450 degrees. Arrange the tomatoes and shallots in a small shallow baking pan; drizzle with 1 tablespoon olive oil. Roast until the edges of the vegetables are golden brown.

2 Combine with the balsamic vinegar, champagne vinegar, 1 tablespoon olive oil, the garlic, basil, oregano, salt and pepper in a blender. Process at high speed for 30 seconds. Add xanthan gum very gradually, processing constantly until thickened to the desired consistency. Spoon into a bowl and refrigerate for 2 hours.

3 Combine the vinaigrette with the mixed greens in a bowl and toss to coat evenly. Serve immediately.

Yields 14 servings

2 vine-ripened tomatoes

2 shallots

1 tablespoon extra-virgin olive oil

1/4 cup balsamic vinegar

2 tablespoons champagne vinegar

1 tablespoon extra-virgin olive oil

2 small garlic cloves

4 fresh basil leaves

1 tablespoon fresh oregano

salt and pepper to taste

xanthan gum to thicken

12 cups mixed greens

nutrition per serving						
CAL	CARB	PRO	FAT	FIBER	CHOL	SOD
26	2g	<1g	2g	<1g	0mg	3mg

Herb-Crusted Salmon with Port Reduction

1   Bring the wine to a boil in a medium saucepan over high heat; the mixture will ignite when it gets very hot, but the flames will die down as it continues to cook. Cook for about 20 minutes or until thickened. Keep warm to serve with the salmon or store in the refrigerator for up to 1 month to serve later.

2   Preheat the oven to 450 degrees. Combine the basil, parsley, tarragon and dill weed in a food processor and process for 30 seconds. Add the panko, olive oil, salt and black pepper and mix well.

3   Rinse the salmon and season on both sides with salt and white pepper. Spray a nonstick ovenproof sauté pan with nonstick cooking spray and heat until smoking. Add the salmon and sear for 45 seconds on each side or until golden brown. Remove to a work surface and coat both sides lightly with the Dijon mustard. Coat with the herbed crumb mixture.

4   Return the salmon to the sauté pan. Place in the oven and bake for about 8 minutes or until medium. Place on 6 serving plates and drizzle with the port reduction. Serve with Saffron Risotto.

Yields 6 servings

1 (750 milliliter) bottle of inexpensive port

1 cup fresh basil leaves

1 cup fresh Italian parsley

1/4 cup fresh tarragon

1/4 cup fresh dill weed

1 cup panko (Japanese bread crumbs)

1 tablespoon extra-virgin olive oil

salt and black pepper to taste

6 (4-ounce) center-cut salmon fillets,
   skinned and deboned

white pepper to taste

2 tablespoons Dijon mustard

Saffron Risotto (page 90)

89

nutrition per serving						
CAL	CARB	PRO	FAT	FIBER	CHOL	SOD
350	21g	26g	11g	1g	62mg	343mg

week two sunday

Saffron Risotto

8 cups chicken stock

salt and white pepper to taste

1/4 cup finely chopped onion

1 teaspoon olive oil

1 teaspoon saffron threads

2 fresh thyme sprigs

2 cups uncooked arborio rice

2 tablespoons dry white wine

1/4 cup light coconut milk

2 tablespoons grated Parmesan cheese

1 Bring the chicken stock to a boil in a medium saucepan. Reduce the heat and add salt and white pepper; maintain at a simmer.

2 Sauté the onion in the olive oil in a saucepan over low heat for 5 minutes or until tender but not brown. Add the saffron, thyme sprigs and rice and cook for 1 to 2 minutes, stirring to coat evenly. Add the wine.

3 Add enough hot stock to cover the rice and cook until the liquid is absorbed, stirring constantly. Repeat the process until the stock is absorbed and the rice is nearly tender. Add the coconut milk and cheese; adjust the seasonings to taste. Cook until the rice is creamy but not runny. Remove and discard the thyme sprigs and serve.

Yields 8 servings

nutrition per serving

CAL	CARB	PRO	FAT	FIBER	CHOL	SOD
247	45g	7g	5g	1g	2mg	661mg

week two sunday

This recipe can also be used to make muffins or quick bread. It can also be served with Warm Berry Compote.

Apple Spice Cake

1¹/₄ cups unbleached flour

²/₃ cup packed brown sugar

1 teaspoon baking powder

¹/₂ teaspoon baking soda

1 teaspoon ground cinnamon

¹/₂ teaspoon ground allspice

2 cups thinly sliced green apples

1 egg

1 egg white

2 tablespoons canola oil

¹/₄ cup strong coffee

¹/₄ cup coffee liqueur

¹/₂ cup dried cranberries

Cinnamon Cream (page 23)

1   Preheat the oven to 350 degrees. Mix the flour, brown sugar, baking powder, baking soda, cinnamon and allspice in a bowl. Make a well in the center of the dry ingredients and add the apples, egg, egg white, canola oil, coffee and liqueur; mix well. Fold in the dried cranberries.

2   Line an 11¹/₂-inch tart pan with a removable bottom with waxed paper and spray with nonstick cooking spray. Add the cake batter and bake for 35 to 40 minutes or until the cake tests done.

3   Cool on a wire rack and place on a serving plate; remove the side. Cut into slices and top each slice with 1 tablespoon Cinnamon Cream.

Yields 12 servings

nutrition per serving						
CAL	CARB	PRO	FAT	FIBER	CHOL	SOD
157	25g	3g	6g	2g	43mg	188mg

week two sunday

monday menu

breakfast

Breakfast Sausage Burrito

lunch

Grilled Turkey on a Baguette with Vegetable Relish and Arugula

Whole Wheat Strawberry Fig Bars

hors d'oeuvre

Sweet Potato Pancakes

dinner

Green and White Asparagus Soup

Seared Atlantic Scallops

with Quinoa Lentil Pilaf and Kabocha Squash Purée

dessert

Almond Ricotta Torte

Breakfast Sausage Burrito

1 Combine the eggs, egg whites, bell pepper, onion, salt and pepper in a bowl and beat to mix well. Pour into a nonstick sauté pan sprayed with nonstick cooking spray and cook until soft-set, stirring frequently.

2 Combine the egg mixture with the sausage, cheese and potato in a bowl and mix well. Spoon the mixture onto the tortillas and fold the tortillas over to enclose the filling. Serve with fresh salsa and avocado, if desired.

Yields 4 servings

4 eggs

4 egg whites

1/4 cup chopped red bell pepper

2 tablespoons chopped onion

salt and pepper to taste

8 ounces turkey sausage, cooked, drained
   and chopped

1/4 cup shredded Monterey Jack cheese or
   Cheddar cheese

1 potato, baked and chopped

4 whole wheat tortillas

nutrition per serving						
CAL	CARB	PRO	FAT	FIBER	CHOL	SOD
351	32g	29g	14g	3g	271mg	760mg

Grilled Turkey on a Baguette with Vegetable Relish and Arugula

Vegetable Relish

1 onion, chopped

1 teaspoon olive oil

2 tablespoons minced garlic

$^1/_2$ cup white wine

$^1/_4$ cup balsamic vinegar

4 cups chopped eggplant

4 cups chopped zucchini or yellow squash

4 cups chopped tomatoes

1 red bell pepper, coarsely chopped

1 tablespoon honey

1 tablespoon capers

$^1/_2$ cup chopped fresh basil

$^1/_2$ cup chopped fresh parsley

2 tablespoons chopped fresh oregano

pinch of dried red chile flakes

1 For the relish, sauté the onion in the olive oil in a saucepan until tender. Add the garlic and sauté for several minutes. Add the wine and vinegar and bring to a boil, stirring to deglaze the saucepan. Cook until reduced by half.

2 Add the eggplant and simmer for 5 minutes. Stir in the zucchini, tomatoes and bell pepper. Cook for 10 minutes. Add the honey, capers, basil, parsley, oregano and chile flakes and simmer until most of the liquid has evaporated.

3 For the turkey, preheat the oven to 475 degrees. Sear the turkey on both sides on a flat grill. Remove to an ovenproof skillet. Roast in the oven for about 15 minutes or until cooked through. Grill the baguette slices on both sides.

4 Place 1 cup of arugula on each serving plate and place 1 baguette slice on the arugula. Top with the turkey and relish. Garnish with a small sprig of fresh basil.

Yields 10 servings

nutrition per serving						
CAL	CARB	PRO	FAT	FIBER	CHOL	SOD
62	12g	3g	1g	3g	3mg	12mg

Turkey

2 pounds turkey tenders

10 diagonal slices sun-dried
   tomato baguette

10 cups fresh arugula

basil sprigs, for garnish

nutrition per serving						
CAL	CARB	PRO	FAT	FIBER	CHOL	SOD
310	37g	31g	5g	7g	55mg	281mg

Whole Wheat Strawberry Fig Bars

1 For the filling, combine the dried strawberries, dried figs, fennel seeds, brown sugar, apple juice and orange juice in a saucepan; mix well. Simmer until thickened, stirring frequently.

2 Cool to room temperature. Process in a food processor or blender until puréed. Spread on a baking sheet lined with baking parchment sprayed with nonstick cooking spray.

3 Place plastic wrap directly on the surface of the mixture and press into a 6×12-inch rectangle 1/4 inch thick. Chill in the refrigerator.

4 For the cookies, mix the whole wheat flour, unbleached flour, baking powder and salt in a bowl. Add the egg, honey, butter and orange zest and mix to form a dough. Wrap with plastic wrap and chill for 1 hour.

5 Preheat the oven to 350 degrees. Divide the chilled dough into 3 portions. Roll each portion into a 6×12-inch rectangle on a floured surface; trim any uneven edges. Cut the filling into three 2-inch strips and lay 1 strip down the center of each rectangle of dough. Fold the sides over the filling and brush with beaten egg white; press lightly to seal.

6 Place on a baking sheet sprayed with nonstick cooking spray. Spray the tops lightly with the nonstick cooking spray and sprinkle with cinnamon. Bake for 25 minutes. Cool on a wire rack and cut each roll into 8 cookies. Garnish with fresh fruit and mint.

Yields 25 (1-bar) servings

Filling

1 cup sliced dried strawberries

1 cup dried figs, stems removed

1/2 teaspoon fennel seeds

1/4 cup packed brown sugar

1/2 cup apple juice

2 tablespoons orange juice

Cookies

2 1/2 cups whole wheat pastry flour

1/2 cup unbleached flour

1 teaspoon baking powder

1 teaspoon salt

1 egg

3/4 cup honey

3 tablespoons butter, softened

grated zest of 1 orange

1 egg white, lightly beaten

ground cinnamon to taste

fresh fruit slices and mint sprigs, for garnish

nutrition per serving						
CAL	CARB	PRO	FAT	FIBER	CHOL	SOD
141	31g	2g	2g	2g	11mg	129mg

Sweet Potato Pancakes

3/4 cup light coconut milk

2 eggs

1 tablespoon vegetable oil

1 1/2 cups unbleached flour

1 1/2 teaspoons baking powder

1 teaspoon salt

1 small red onion, chopped

2 tablespoons chopped parsley

1 sweet potato or yam

sour cream and Italian parsley, for garnish

1 Combine the coconut milk, eggs and oil in a blender and process until smooth. Add the flour, baking powder and salt and mix well. Combine with the onion and parsley in a bowl and mix well. Let the batter stand for about 1 hour.

2 Peel and grate the sweet potato and stir into the batter when ready to cook. Ladle about 1 tablespoon of the batter at a time into a nonstick sauté pan sprayed with nonstick cooking spray. Cook until golden brown on both sides.

3 Remove to a plate and garnish with sour cream and parsley. Serve immediately.

Yields 8 servings

nutrition per serving						
CAL	CARB	PRO	FAT	FIBER	CHOL	SOD
152	21g	4g	5g	1g	49mg	365mg

Green and White Asparagus Soup

1 Cut off the tips of the green asparagus and cut the stems into small pieces. Sauté half the onion in half the olive oil in a saucepan for 5 minutes or until tender. Add the green asparagus and stir to coat evenly. Stir in half the flour and cook for several minutes, stirring constantly.

2 Add half the coconut milk and half the stock, or just enough stock to cover the asparagus. Bring to a boil and reduce the heat, stirring constantly. Simmer for 5 to 10 minutes.

3 Process the mixture in a blender at high speed for 1 minute. Strain through a strainer or large china cap. Season with half the Splenda, salt and white pepper.

4 Repeat the entire process in a separate saucepan using the white asparagus and the remaining ingredients. Pour each soup into separate measuring cups. Pour carefully into opposite sides of soup bowls in a curvilinear pattern, taking care not to mix.

Yields 12 servings

1 bunch green asparagus

1 yellow onion, chopped

2 tablespoons pomace olive oil

1/4 cup unbleached flour

1/4 cup light coconut milk

3 cups chicken stock

2 teaspoons Splenda

salt and white pepper to taste

1 bunch white asparagus

nutrition per serving						
CAL	CARB	PRO	FAT	FIBER	CHOL	SOD
50	5g	1g	3g	1g	<1mg	300mg

To retain the green color in the green asparagus soup, cool it in an ice bath after you purée it and chill until cool. Reheat it to serve and serve immediately.

This is a perfect summertime dish. Our presentation is typical of Cal-a-Vie cuisine. We recommend cooking the scallops medium-rare if not serving immediately. You can finish them at the last minute to medium or medium-well. The squash purée can be served at room temperature.

Seared Atlantic Scallops with Quinoa Lentil Pilaf and Kabocha Squash Purée

Quinoa Lentil Pilaf

12 ounces uncooked quinoa

1/4 cup lemon juice

2 tablespoons olive oil

1 cup cooked lentils or beans

3 tablespoons minced fresh mint

1 cup minced fresh parsley

1/3 cup chopped green onions

1 cup chopped cucumber

1 tablespoon minced garlic

1/2 teaspoon sea salt

Kabocha Squash Purée

1 kabocha squash

salt and pepper to taste

Scallops

18 large sea scallops

salt and pepper to taste

1   For the pilaf, cook the quinoa in salted water in a saucepan for 10 minutes or until tender; drain and remove to a bowl. Cool to room temperature. Add the lemon juice, olive oil, lentils, mint, parsley, green onions, cucumber and garlic. Season with the sea salt and mix well. Chill until serving time.

2   For the squash, preheat the oven to 400 degrees. Cut the squash into halves and remove and discard the seeds. Place the squash on a baking sheet. Roast the squash until tender; cool to room temperature. Scoop the pulp into a food processor. Process until puréed. Mix with salt and pepper in a bowl.

3   For the scallops, season the scallops with salt and pepper. Sear on both sides in a sauté pan until cooked through.

4   To assemble, spoon 1 cup of the quinoa mixture into the centers of 6 plates. Place 3 tablespoonfuls of the squash purée around the quinoa. Place 1 scallop on the top of each dollop of squash purée.

Yields 6 servings

week two monday

		nutrition per serving				
CAL	CARB	PRO	FAT	FIBER	CHOL	SOD
270	38g	16g	7g	7g	15mg	360mg

Almond Ricotta Torte

1   Preheat the oven to 375 degrees. Process the almonds in a food processor until coarsely ground. Add the graham crackers and process until finely crushed. Add the egg yolks, ricotta cheese, flour, fructose, lemon zest, vanilla and almond extract; process to mix well.

2   Beat the egg whites in a mixing bowl until stiff peaks form. Fold into the batter. Spoon into a 1-quart soufflé dish well sprayed with nonstick cooking spray.

3   Bake for about 40 minutes or until set. Cool in the baking dish for 20 minutes; the torte will sink slightly. Remove to a serving plate and slice into wedges to serve. Serve with glazed fresh berries or a drizzle of Chocolate Fondue (page 44) and a fanned sliced strawberry.

Yields 12 servings

1/3 cup toasted almonds

2 honey graham crackers

2 egg yolks

15 ounces extra-skim ricotta cheese or low-fat cottage cheese

3 tablespoons flour

1/4 cup fructose

grated zest of 1 lemon

1 teaspoon vanilla extract

1/4 teaspoon almond extract

4 egg whites

nutrition per serving						
CAL	CARB	PRO	FAT	FIBER	CHOL	SOD
127	14g	8g	4g	<1g	37mg	86mg

therapeutic treatments

Cal-a-Vie offers a therapy program unlike any other in the country, utilizing sophisticated European techniques of thalassotherapy, hydrotherapy, and aromatherapy. These sensible therapeutic treatments help restore your body to its natural balance. Inner serenity returns, and you feel relaxed, content, and deliciously pampered.

Hot Stone Massage

Melt away your stress as heated basalt lava stones glide effortlessly along your body. The heat from the stones relaxes the muscles deeply and allows the therapist to break down contracted muscle fibers, leaving you with a feeling of total relief and relaxation.

Hydrotherapy

Enjoy a therapeutic underwater massage in multi-jet tubs using various seaweeds and essential oils. The effect is slimming, relaxing, and invigorating.

Magnetic Therapy

Muscles are stimulated with a magnetic roller, and the therapist uses finger or palm pressure to assist in movement of energy. Blood circulation is increased, which helps reduce pain and speed of healing of tired, sore, or tense bodies. This is an exceptional treatment for those who are muscular and who exercise frequently.

Massage

Skilled therapists, trained in the art of Swedish, massage, Shiatsu massage, and other bodywork techniques, perform claming yet energizing massage.

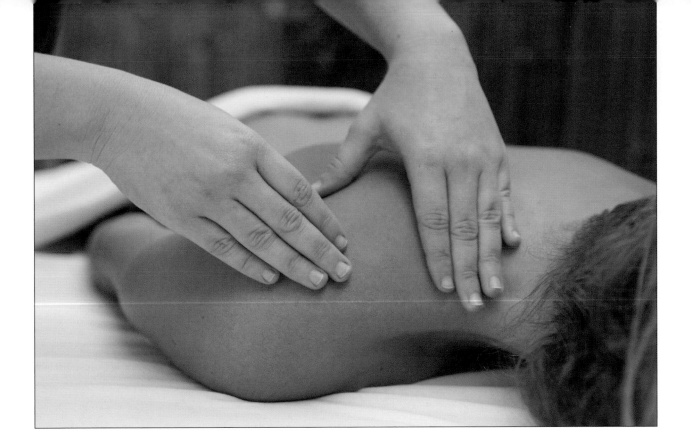

Reflexology Massage

A specialized foot massage that stimulates body function and relaxation. This centuries-old technique will leave you feeling calm yet invigorated.

Thalassotherapy

This seaweed wrap uses seaweed harvested off the coast of Brittany in France. All the nutrients are preserved in powdered form until activated with warm water to make a warm, rich paste to smooth all over the body. You are then cocooned in a thermal blanket. The warmth helps you to absorb all the vitamins and minerals inherent in seaweed, as well as to detoxify your system. All the while, a therapist is relaxing you with a soothing face and scalp massage.

tuesday menu

breakfast

Praline Pancakes

lunch

Baja Bass Bake with Roasted Chiles

Low-Calorie Butter Cookies

hors d'oeuvre

Grilled Chicken Satay

dinner

Heirloom Tomato and Fresh Mozzarella Salad

Lobster Ravioli with Wild Mushroom Sauce

dessert

Blueberry Cobbler

Praline Pancakes

1 Mix the flour, baking powder, nutmeg, Splenda and salt in a large bowl. Add the milk, butter, Grand Marnier and vanilla and stir until smooth. Stir in the pecans and rice. Fold in the egg whites.

2 Spray a griddle with butter-flavor nonstick cooking spray. Ladle about 1/4 cup of the batter at a time onto the griddle. Cook over medium heat until bubbles form. Turn the pancakes over and cook until golden brown. Garnish with confectioners' sugar and fresh fruit and drizzle with warm syrup.

Yields 6 servings

1 cup unbleached flour

1 teaspoon baking powder

1/4 teaspoon nutmeg or ground cinnamon

2 tablespoons Splenda or sugar

1/4 teaspoon salt

1 1/2 cups fat-free milk

1 tablespoon melted butter or almond oil

1 tablespoon Grand Marnier

2 teaspoons vanilla extract

1/3 cup toasted chopped pecans

1 cup cooked brown rice or cooked white rice

4 egg whites, stiffly beaten

confectioners' sugar, fresh fruit and warm syrup, for garnish

103

nutrition per serving

CAL	CARB	PRO	FAT	FIBER	CHOL	SOD
212	31g	8g	5g	2g	1mg	272mg

Baja Bass Bake with Roasted Chiles

1 (3-ounce) fillet sea bass

1 teaspoon chili powder

1 pasilla chile

4 tomatillos, cut into quarters

kernels from 1 ear of corn

2 tablespoons chopped red bell pepper

1 garlic clove, minced

1 tablespoon chopped red onion

1 tablespoon chopped cilantro

1/4 teaspoon cumin

1/8 teaspoon salt

1 teaspoon olive oil

1 sprig of cilantro and 1 lemon wedge,
   for garnish

1 Preheat the oven to 450 degrees. Rub the fish with the chili powder. Place on a baking sheet sprayed with nonstick cooking spray. Bake for 15 to 20 minutes or until the fish is cooked through.

2 Roast the chile over an open flame until blackened. Remove and discard the skin and seeds. Sauté the tomatillos, corn, bell pepper, garlic, onion and cilantro with the cumin and salt in the olive oil in a sauté pan for 10 minutes or until tender.

3 Spoon onto a serving plate. Top with the fish and garnish with cilantro and a lemon wedge. Serve with the chile.

Yields 1 serving

nutrition per serving						
CAL	CARB	PRO	FAT	FIBER	CHOL	SOD
255	24g	24g	8g	4g	24mg	358mg

Low-Calorie Butter Cookies

1 Preheat the oven to 400 degrees. Cream the butter and sugar in a mixing bowl until light and fluffy. Beat in the egg whites and vanilla. Add the flour and baking powder gradually, mixing to form a dough.

2 Drop by teaspoonfuls onto a cookie sheet sprayed with nonstick cooking spray; press with the back of a spoon to flatten. Bake for 10 minutes. Cool on the cookie sheet for several minutes and remove to a wire rack to cool completely.

Yields 30 cookies

1/3 cup butter, softened

1/2 cup sugar

2 egg whites

1 teaspoon vanilla exract

2 cups unbleached flour

1 teaspoon baking powder

nutrition per serving						
CAL	CARB	PRO	FAT	FIBER	CHOL	SOD
59	9g	1g	2g	<1g	5mg	34mg

Grilled Chicken Satay

1 Combine the stock, lime juice, garlic, ginger, salt and pepper in a bowl and mix well. Add the chicken and stir to coat evenly. Marinate, covered, in the refrigerator for 1 hour; drain and discard the marinade.

2 Thread each chicken strip onto a skewer. Grill for 6 minutes or until cooked through. Garnish with lime zest and serve with a spicy sauce.

3 You can also serve chicken satay with steamed rice as a lunch entrée. As an option to grilling, you can roast the chicken skewers in the oven or wrap them in foil and bake them.

Yields 8 servings

1/4 cup chicken stock or vegetable stock

1/4 cup lime juice

3 garlic cloves, minced

1 teaspoon ginger

salt and pepper to taste

4 boneless skinless chicken breasts,
   cut into strips (about 1 pound)

grated lime zest, for garnish

nutrition per serving						
CAL	CARB	PRO	FAT	FIBER	CHOL	SOD
67	1g	13g	1g	<1g	33mg	59mg

The tomatoes should be marinated for at least 4 hours for maximum flavor. Serve with a warm crusty baguette to clean up all the remaining balsamic reduction.

Heirloom Tomato and Fresh Mozzarella Salad

5 ripe medium heirloom tomatoes, sliced
   1/2 inch thick

1/4 cup finely chopped shallots

1 tablespoon granulated garlic

2/3 cup champagne vinegar

2 tablespoons extra-virgin olive oil

kosher salt and freshly cracked pepper
   to taste

1 (4-ounce) ball fresh mozzarella cheese
   in liquid, about 2 to 3 inches wide

1/2 cup Balsamic Reduction (below)

1 tablespoon chopped fresh basil

1 Arrange the tomato slices in a single layer in a 9×13-inch glass dish. Sprinkle evenly with the shallots, garlic, vinegar, olive oil, salt and pepper. Marinate in the refrigerator for 4 to 12 hours.

2 Drain the tomato slices and drizzle with the balsamic reduction and basil. Cut the mozzarella cheese into slices the same width as the tomatoes. Alternate 3 tomato slices with 2 cheese slices in a circle on serving plates. Serve cold.

Yields 6 servings

nutrition per serving						
CAL	CARB	PRO	FAT	FIBER	CHOL	SOD
94	5g	3g	7g	1g	11mg	30mg

Balsamic Reduction

16 ounces moderately-priced
   balsamic vinegar

2 shallots

1 Combine the vinegar with the shallots in a large saucepan. Cook until the mixture is reduced to about 2 ounces, stirring frequently and watching carefully as the mixture begins to thicken to prevent burning.

2 Remove the shallots and cool to room temperature. Store in the refrigerator for up to 1 month.

Yields 32 servings

nutrition per serving						
CAL	CARB	PRO	FAT	FIBER	CHOL	SOD
10	2g	<1g	<1g	0g	0mg	4mg

Lobster Ravioli with Wild Mushroom Sauce

Mushroom Sauce

1 teaspoon olive oil

1 shallot, minced

1 garlic clove, minced

1/4 cup crimini mushrooms, sliced
   1/4 inch thick

1/4 cup oyster mushrooms, sliced

1/4 cup shiitake mushrooms, stemmed
   and sliced

1/2 teaspoon salt (optional)

1/4 teaspoon pepper

1/4 cup white wine

1/4 cup vegetable stock or roasted
   chicken stock

Ravioli

15 vegetable-filled ravioli (without cheese)

3 ounces lobster, shrimp or seasoned
   tofu, sliced

1 tablespoon minced Italian parsley

1 For the sauce, heat the olive oil in a heavy skillet. Add the shallot, garlic and mushrooms and sauté for several minutes. Season with the salt and pepper and stir in the wine and stock. Simmer until of the desired consistency.

2 For the ravioli, cook the pasta al dente in water in a saucepan; drain. Spoon 5 ravioli onto each serving plate. Spoon the mushroom sauce over the ravioli and top with the lobster and minced parsley.

Yields 3 servings

nutrition per serving						
CAL	CARB	PRO	FAT	FIBER	CHOL	SOD
204	25g	13g	5g	2g	40mg	634mg

The basis of this cobbler is a sponge cake known as a génoise. It was originally developed in Genoa, Italy, and adapted by the French.

Blueberry Cobbler

1   Purée 1 cup of the blueberries in a blender or food processor. Strain into a bowl and add the remaining blueberries, honey and lemon zest; mix well.

2   Preheat the oven to 350 degrees. Whisk the eggs with the fructose, cardamom and nutmeg in a metal mixing bowl over a pan of simmering water until the mixture reaches 120 degrees, or is hot to the touch. Remove from the heat and beat until tripled in volume and the bottom of the bowl is cool to the touch.

3   Whisk in the vanilla and fold in the flour gently. Spoon 1 heaping tablespoonful of the batter into each of 12 small ramekins or soufflé dishes lightly sprayed with nonstick cooking spray.

4   Bake until puffy, firm and golden brown. Spoon 2 tablespoonfuls of the blueberry mixture over each cobbler to serve.

Yields 12 servings

2 cups fresh blueberries or thawed
   frozen blueberries

1 teaspoon honey

1 tablespoon finely grated lemon zest

2 eggs

$1/3$ cup granulated fructose or sugar

$1/4$ teaspoon cardamom

$1/8$ teaspoon nutmeg

1 teaspoon vanilla extract

$1/2$ cup sifted unbleached flour or whole
   wheat pastry flour, sifted

109

nutrition per serving

CAL	CARB	PRO	FAT	FIBER	CHOL	SOD
68	13g	2g	1g	1g	41mg	12mg

wednesday menu

breakfast

Brioche French Toast with Apple Custard Cream

lunch

Tandoori Chicken

Roasted Vegetables

Roasted Red Bell Pepper Hummus

Cottage Cheese Spread

Naan Bread

Blueberry Mousse

hors d'oeuvre

Creole Crab Cakes

dinner

Haricot Vert Salad

Bluenose Sea Bass and Braised Vegetables Provençal

dessert

Banana Ricotta Napoleon

Brioche French Toast with Apple Custard Cream

1 For the custard cream, beat the eggs with the sugar, vanilla, cinnamon and salt in a bowl. Heat the milk in a double boiler over gently simmering water until tiny bubbles form around the edge. Whisk the milk into the egg mixture very gradually.

2 Return the mixture to the double boiler and cook over low heat until thickened, whisking constantly. Stir in the applesauce and lemon zest; keep warm.

3 For the French toast, beat the eggs and egg whites with the milk, vanilla, cinnamon and salt in a bowl. Heat a nonstick skillet sprayed with nonstick cooking spray.

4 Dip the bread slices into the egg mixture, allowing them to soak up some of the eggs. Place in the skillet and cook until golden brown on both sides. Serve the toast with the custard cream and garnish with confectioners' sugar and fresh mint.

Yields 6 servings

Apple Custard Cream

2 eggs

2 tablespoons sugar or Splenda

1 teaspoon vanilla extract

1/4 teaspoon ground cinnamon

salt to taste

1 cup 1% milk

1/2 cup applesauce or chopped fresh apple

1 teaspoon grated lemon zest

French Toast

3 eggs

2 egg whites

1/2 cup 1% milk

1 teaspoon vanilla extract

1/2 teaspoon cinnamon

1/4 teaspoon salt

6 (1/2- to 3/4-inch) slices brioche or
    French bread

confectioners' sugar and fresh mint,
    for garnish

111

nutrition per serving						
CAL	CARB	PRO	FAT	FIBER	CHOL	SOD
293	43g	14g	6g	2g	177mg	622mg

Tandoori Chicken is perfect for lunch or dinner. Roll it in Naan Bread for sandwiches or allow guests to build sandwiches to order and serve with spreads such as Roasted Red Pepper Hummus or Cottage Cheese Spread.

Tandoori Chicken

1 tablespon extra-virgin olive oil

2 tablespoons fresh lemon juice

3/4 cup nonfat plain yogurt

3/4 cup chopped yellow onion

1 tablespoon chopped garlic

1 tablespoon peeled fresh ginger

1 tablespoon paprika

1 teaspoon turmeric

1 teaspoon cumin

1 teaspoon garam masala

1 teaspoon coriander

1 tablespoon cayenne pepper

6 (5-ounce) boneless chicken breasts

salt and black pepper to taste

1   Combine the olive oil, lemon juice, yogurt, onion, garlic and ginger in a blender and process at high speed until puréed. Add the paprika, tumeric, cumin, garam masala, coriander and cayenne pepper and process for 30 seconds longer. Remove to a bowl.

2   Score the chicken lightly with a sharp knife to allow the marinade to penetrate and add to the marinade. Marinate in the refrigerator for 2 to 12 hours.

3   Preheat the oven to 500 degrees. Drain and discard the marinade and season the chicken on both sides with salt and black pepper. Place on a baking sheet and insert a meat thermometer into the thickest portion. Roast for 20 to 25 minutes or until the internal temperature reaches 155 degrees on the thermometer, or until nearly cooked through. Let stand for 5 minutes or until the internal temperature reaches 160 degrees.

Yields 6 servings

nutrition per serving

CAL	CARB	PRO	FAT	FIBER	CHOL	SOD
212	7g	35g	5g	2g	83mg	112mg

Roasted Vegetables

2 carrots, peeled

2 Japanese eggplant

2 yellow squash

2 zucchini

1 fennel bulb

1 red bell pepper

1/2 red onion

2 tablespoons extra-virgin olive oil

salt and pepper to taste

1   Preheat the oven to 400 degrees. Rinse the carrots, eggplant, squash, zucchini, fennel, bell pepper and onion under cold water and allow to air dry.

2   Cut the vegetables into 3-inch pieces, discarding the ends. Combine with the olive oil in a bowl and season with salt and pepper.

3   Line a baking sheet with baking parchment sprayed with nonstick cooking spray. Roast until the vegetables begin to brown. Stir and roast until evenly brown. Cool to room temperature and serve or chill until serving time and serve chilled.

Yields 6 servings

nutrition per serving

CAL	CARB	PRO	FAT	FIBER	CHOL	SOD
147	25g	4g	5g	8g	0mg	33mg

Roasted Red Bell Pepper Hummus

1 Preheat the oven to 450 degrees. Place the bell peppers on a baking sheet and roast until the skin is charred. Place in a bowl, cover with plastic wrap and let stand for 30 minutes. Remove and dscard the skin and seeds; reserve any accumulated liquid.

2 Combine the undrained garbanzo beans, garlic, paprika, cumin, coriander, white pepper and black pepper in a medium saucepan. Cook until the liquid evaporates.

3 Process in a food processor for 1 minute or until smooth, adding the olive oil, tahini, lemon juice, salt, roasted peppers and accumulated pepper liquid. Process for 1 minute longer. Spoon into a bowl and chill until serving time.

Yields 6 servings

2 large red bell peppers

1 (15-ounce) can garbanzo beans

3 garlic cloves

1 tablespoon paprika

1 tablespoon cumin

1 teaspoon coriander

1 teaspoon white pepper

1 teaspoon black pepper

1 tablespoon extra-virgin olive oil

1 tablespoon tahini (sesame paste)

1/4 cup lemon juice

salt to taste

nutrition per serving						
CAL	CARB	PRO	FAT	FIBER	CHOL	SOD
108	15g	4g	4g	5g	0mg	218mg

Cottage Cheese Spread

Combine the cottage cheese, onion, chives, paprika and turmeric in a medium bowl and fold together with a spatula. Chill until serving time.

Yields 6 servings

1 cup low-fat small curd cottage cheese

1/4 cup finely chopped onion

2 tablespoons finely chopped chives

1/2 teaspoon paprika

1/4 teaspoon turmeric

nutrition per serving						
CAL	CARB	PRO	FAT	FIBER	CHOL	SOD
31	2g	5g	<1g	<1g	2mg	153mg

Naan Bread

1 teaspoon dry yeast

1/2 teaspoon Splenda

1/2 cup warm (110-degree) water

1/2 cup (or more) all-purpose flour

1/2 cup whole wheat pastry flour

1/2 teaspoon salt

1 tablespoon vegetable oil

2 tablespoons nonfat plain yogurt

olive oil or nonstick cooking spray

nutrition per serving						
CAL	CARB	PRO	FAT	FIBER	CHOL	SOD
87	14g	3g	3g	1g	<1mg	199mg

1 Dissove the yeast and the Splenda in the warm water in a glass measuring cup. Let stand for 7 to 10 minutes or until foamy. Sift the all-purpose flour, whole wheat flour and salt into a bowl and make a well in the center. Pour the yeast mixture, oil and yogurt into the well. Mix gently with the hands to form a dough, adding additional flour if necessary.

2 Knead on a floured surface for 5 minutes. Place in a lightly oiled bowl, turning to coat the surface. Cover with plastic and let rise in a warm place for 1 hour or until doubled in bulk.

3 Roll into 6-inch circles on a floured surface and brush with olive oil or spray with nonstick cooking spray. Grill over medium heat until golden brown on both sides. Serve immediately.

Yields 6 servings

Blueberry Mousse

1 Chill the bowl of a food processor. Combine the frozen blueberries, crème de cassis, orange juice, honey, banana, vanilla and protein powder in the chilled bowl and process for 4 to 5 minutes or until thick and smooth.

2 Spoon into 12 chilled champagne glasses and garnish each glass with 3 fresh blueberries. Serve immediately or freeze to serve later.

Yields 12 servings

2 1/2 cups frozen blueberries

2 teaspoons crème de cassis

1/2 cup orange juice

2 tablespoons honey

1/2 ripe banana

1/4 teaspoon vanilla extract

1/2 cup protein powder

36 fresh blueberries, for garnish

nutrition per serving						
CAL	CARB	PRO	FAT	FIBER	CHOL	SOD
29	7g	1g	<1g	<1g	<1mg	10mg

week two wednesday

Creole Crab Cakes

1 pound lump blue crab meat, drained

1 egg

1 teaspoon Dijon mustard

2 tablespoons nonfat mayonnaise

1/3 cup panko (Japanese bread crumbs)

1 tablespoon chopped Italian parsley

1 teapoon Cajun seasoning

panko for coating the crab cakes

1 teaspoon olive oil

1 Combine the crab meat, egg, Dijon mustard, mayonnaise, 1/3 cup panko, the parsley and Cajun seasoning in a bowl and mix well. Chill for 10 minutes. Shape into cakes with a 1-ounce ice cream scoop. Coat lightly with additional panko.

2 Preheat the oven to 450 degrees. Spray a nonstick sauté pan with nonstick cooking spray and add the olive oil. Add the crab cakes and cook until golden brown on both sides. Place in the oven and bake for 5 to 7 minutes or until cooked through.

Yields 12 servings

nutrition per serving

CAL	CARB	PRO	FAT	FIBER	CHOL	SOD
59	3g	8g	2g	<1g	46mg	164mg

week two wednesday

Haricot Vert Salad

1 Bring a saucepan of salted water to a boil and add the beans. Cook just until tender-crisp. Remove to a large bowl of ice water with a slotted spoon to stop the cooking.

2 Add the asparagus tips to the water in the saucepan and cook just until blanched. Remove to the ice water to cool; drain. Chill the beans and asparagus tips until serving time.

3 Combine the beans and asparagus tips with the tomatoes, shallot, salt and pepper in a bowl. Add 1/2 cup of the Tarragon Vinaigrette and mix lightly. Spoon onto 6 chilled serving plates.

4 Mix the remaining Vinaigrette with the frisée in a bowl and toss to coat evenly. Spoon onto the bean mixture and serve immediately.

Yields 6 servings

salt to taste

1 pound fresh haricots verts (green beans)

1 cup diagonally cut fresh green asparagus tips

1 cup diagonally cut fresh white asparagus tips

3/4 cup cherry tomato halves

1 large shallot, finely chopped

salt and pepper to taste

1/2 cup Tarragon Vinaigrette (below)

3 cups frisée or mixed greens

nutrition per serving						
CAL	CARB	PRO	FAT	FIBER	CHOL	SOD
54	10g	3g	1g	3g	0mg	22mg

Tarragon Vinaigrette

Combine the olive oil, vinegar, ice water, Dijon mustard, shallot, garlic, xanthan gum, salt and pepper in a blender. Process for 1 minute or until smooth. Add the tarragon and pulse just until mixed. Store in the refrigerator.

Yields 1 3/4 cups

2 tablespoons extra-virgin olive oil

1/3 cup sherry vinegar

2 cups ice water

1 teaspoon Dijon mustard

1 large shallot, chopped

2 small garlic cloves

1/2 teaspoon xanthan gum

salt and pepper to taste

2 tablespoons chopped fresh tarragon

nutrition per serving						
CAL	CARB	PRO	FAT	FIBER	CHOL	SOD
49	1g	<1g	5g	<1g	0mg	50mg

Bluenose Sea Bass and
Braised Vegetables Provençal

Braised Vegetables

8 baby carrots

8 fennel bulbs, trimmed and sliced
   lengthwise

4 artichoke bottoms, cut into quarters

8 cipollini or pearl onions

12 fingerling potatoes, blanched al dente

2 tablespoons olive oil

1 tablespoon chopped garlic

1/4 cup Pernod

4 cups chicken stock

salt and white pepper to taste

1 Roma tomato, chopped

Sea Bass

4 (3-ounce) portions fresh bluenose
   sea bass

salt and pepper to taste

1 For the vegetables, sauté the carrots, fennel, artichoke bottoms, cipollini and potatoes separately in a nonstick sauté pan until seared but not cooked through. Remove the fennel and potatoes to a bowl. Remove carrots, artichokes and cipollini to a separate bowl.

2 Add the olive oil and garlic to the same sauté pan and sweat over low heat for about 2 minutes; do not brown. Add the Pernod and cook until most of the liquid evaporates.

3 Add the fennel, potatoes and stock. Simmer until the fennel is tender. Add the artichokes, carrots and cipollini. Simmer until tender. Season with salt and white pepper and stir in the tomato. You can thicken the mixture with a slurry of arrowroot and water if needed for the desired consistency.

4 For the fish, pat the fillets dry and season with salt and white pepper. Grill for 3 to 4 minutes on each side or until firm.

5 Spoon the vegetables into 4 large bowls with a slotted spoon. Place the fish on the vegetables and spoon the vegetable broth generously over the top.

Yields 4 servings

		nutrition per serving				
CAL	CARB	PRO	FAT	FIBER	CHOL	SOD
421	59g	24g	10g	8g	40mg	761mg

The leftover phyllo dough can be used for turnovers with a fruit or ricotta filling. Cut the phyllo into squares, fill half the square with the filling and fold the phyllo over to form a triangle. Seal with a wash made of egg white and a little water and bake until golden brown.

Banana Ricotta Napolean

1 Preheat the oven to 350 degrees. Layer 3 sheets of the phyllo dough on a baking sheet with 1/2-inch sides. Spray the layers with nonstick cooking spray and sprinkle with some of the graham cracker crumbs and cinnamon. Repeat the process 3 more times to use all the phyllo dough and graham cracker crumbs.

2 Cut the layers into eight 2×3-inch rectangles, removing the unused portions of the dough from the baking sheet and reserving for another use. Bake for 10 minutes or until golden brown.

3 Combine the cheese, confectioners' sugar and vanilla in a bowl and mix well. Place 1 baked phyllo stack on each of 4 serving plates. Spread each with 1 tablespoon of the ricotta mixture and top with 2 slices of banana and 1 sliced strawberry. Spread with a second tablespoon of the ricotta mixture and top with a second baked phyllo square.

4 Drizzle each serving with Chocolate Fondue in a zigzag pattern. Garnish with mint and raspberries.

Yields 4 servings

9 sheets phyllo dough

1/2 cup graham cracker crumbs

1 teaspoon ground cinnamon

1/2 cup nonfat ricotta cheese or vanilla
 yogurt cheese

1 tablespoon confectioners' sugar

1 teaspoon vanilla extract

1 banana, cut into 8 slices

4 large strawberries, sliced

2 tablespoons Chocolate Fondue (page 44)

4 sprigs mint

12 fresh raspberries

119

nutrition per serving						
CAL	CARB	PRO	FAT	FIBER	CHOL	SOD
246	41g	6g	7g	3g	5mg	238mg

Throughout the year, Cal-a-Vie offers weeklong sojourns that focus on specific elements of personal wellness. If yoga, pilates, women's health, or culinary arts particularly interest you, the spa provides intensives in each of these areas and more.

Beauty Week

This inspiring week includes rejuvenating beauty treatments, makeovers, and hair and makeup treatments.

Culinary Week

Join our executive chef, as well as other renowned experts, for a week of daily cooking classes, and learn tips on nutritious cooking.

Pilates Week

Join top experts in Cal-a-Vie's pilates studio for inspiration, encouragement, and, most importantly, a week of exercise accessible to all. Watch for special guest instructors during these intensive weeks.

Tennis Week

Whatever your tennis level may be, this week will prove to be a memorable tennis experience! Guests have the opportunity to participate in tennis clinics hosted by professionals. A combination of fundamentals, strategy, and match play will lift your game to a new level, while you enjoy all the benefits that an on-court workout provides.

Women's Wellness Week

Interact with top healthcare experts as they share the latest insights on a variety of health issues including menopause, osteoporosis, plastic surgery, stress, and cardiovascular disease.

Yoga Week

The healing benefits of this popular meditative practice will change your lifestyle. A variety of levels are offered, so beginners and well-seasoned practitioners alike are invited to join us. Often, guest instructors come for the week to share their expertise in specialty areas such as progressive power yoga.

theme weeks

thursday menu

breakfast

Smoked Salmon and Spring Onion Omelet

lunch

Tuscan Lasagna

Strawberry Shortcake

hors d'oeuvre

Heirloom Tomato Hummus

Pita

dinner

Corn Chowder

Grilled Duck with Caramelized Figs

dessert

Piña Colada Sorbet

Smoked Salmon and Spring Onion Omelet

1 Preheat the oven to 400 degrees. Beat the eggs with the egg whites in a bowl.

2 Spray a nonstick omelet pan with nonstick cooking spray or brush with oil. Add 1/4 of the egg mixture to the pan and cook until the eggs begin to set. Top with 1 ounce of the salmon, 1 tablespoon of the sour cream and 1 tablespoon of the spring onions.

3 Place in the oven and bake for about 5 minutes or until cooked through. Remove from the oven and fold over to enclose the filling. Repeat with the remaining ingredients. Garnish with fresh berries and a sprinkle of chives or spring onions.

Yields 4 servings

4 eggs

4 egg whites

nonstick cooking spray or vegetable oil

4 ounces smoked salmon

1/4 cup light sour cream

1/4 cup thinly sliced spring onions
   or scallions

fresh berries and chives or spring onions,
   for garnish

nutrition per serving

CAL	CARB	PRO	FAT	FIBER	CHOL	SOD
165	3g	16g	9g	<1g	228mg	714mg

This dish tastes so good and is so much lower in fat than regular lasagna that some of our guests can't believe it can be "spa food." A helpful hint when preparing it at home is to allow it to cool completely and then chilling it in the refrigerator. Reheat it at 325 degrees for 1 hour or until hot in the center and let stand for at least 10 minutes before serving.

Tuscan Lasagna

salt to taste

vegetable oil

1 pound fresh or dried lasagna noodles

4 cups Turkey Tomato Bolognese Sauce
   (page 43)

3 cups Spa Béchamel Sauce (page 125)

1/2 cup Herbed Crumbs (page 125)

2 tablespoons grated
   Parmigiano-Reggiano

1 cup shredded part-skim
   mozzarella cheese

1   Preheat the oven to 375 degrees. Spray a 9×13-inch baking dish lightly with nonstick cooking spray. Bring enough water to cover the noodles to a boil in a saucepan and add salt to taste and a small amount of oil. Add the noodles and cook al dente; drain. Place in ice water to stop the cooking and drain again.

2   Spread a thin layer of the Turkey Tomato Bolognese Sauce in the prepared baking dish and arrange a layer of noodles over the sauce. Spread a thin layer of the Spa Béchamel Sauce over the noodles and sprinkle with a layer of the Herbed Crumbs, Parmigiano-Reggiano and mozzarella cheese.

3   Repeat the process 2 or 3 times and finish with a layer of the Turkey Tomato Bolognese Sauce, cheeses and Herbed Crumbs. Wrap the dish with plastic wrap and foil and bake for 1 hour. Let stand for 10 to 15 minutes before serving.

4   Nutritional analysis includes the Spa Béchamel Sauce and the Herbed Crumbs.

Yields 8 servings

nutrition per serving						
CAL	CARB	PRO	FAT	FIBER	CHOL	SOD
257	36g	15g	5g	2g	27mg	290mg

Spa Béchamel Sauce

1 Combine the milk, onion, nutmeg and cracked black pepper in a medium saucepan. Bring to a boil and strain through a china cap into another medium saucepan. Bring to a simmer.

2 Blend the flour with the water to make a slurry. Whisk gradually into the simmering milk mixture . Cook until thickened and smooth, whisking constantly. Season with salt and white pepper. Remove from the heat and let stand for 15 to 20 minutes before using.

3 A slurry is a quick way to thicken a sauce without a roux or added fat.

Yields 3 cups

3 cups nonfat milk

1/2 cup chopped yellow onion

1/8 teaspoon nutmeg

1 teaspoon cracked black pepper

1/2 cup flour

3/4 cup water

salt and white pepper to taste

Herbed Crumbs

1 Combine the basil, parsley and tarragon in a food processor and process for 30 seconds.

2 Combine with the panko, olive oil, salt and pepper in a bowl and mix well.

Yields 3 cups

1 cup fresh basil leaves

1 cup fresh Italian parsley

1/4 cup fresh tarragon

1 cup panko (Japanese bread crumbs)

1 tablespoon extra-virgin olive oil

salt and pepper to taste

week two thursday

Strawberry Shortcake

2 eggs

3/4 cup granulated fructose or sugar

1/4 teaspoon cardamom

grated nutmeg to taste

1/4 teaspoon vanilla extract

1/2 cup all-purpose flour

12 ounces Orange Yogurt Cream

12 large strawberries

confectioners' sugar, for garnish

nutrition per serving

CAL	CARB	PRO	FAT	FIBER	CHOL	SOD
138	27g	6g	1g	1g	37mg	69mg

1 Preheat the oven to 350 degrees. Combine the eggs, fructose, cardamom and nutmeg in a metal mixing bowl; mix well. Place over a pan of simmering water and cook to 120 degrees or until hot to the touch, whisking constantly and taking care not to scramble the eggs.

2 Remove from the heat and beat at high speed until the mixture is tripled in volume and the bowl is completely cool to the touch. Whisk in the vanilla. Sift the flour over the batter and fold in carefully with a spatula or whisk. Spoon into 12 muffin cups sprayed with nonstick cooking spray. Bake for 10 minutes or until puffed and golden brown. Remove to a wire rack to cool.

3 Split the cakes into halves horizontally. Spoon the Orange Yogurt Cream into a pastry bag fitted with a small star tip. Pipe 1 ounce of the cream onto the bottom half of each cake. Cut each strawberry into thin slices and layer 1 strawberry over each cake. Replace the tops of the cakes and sprinkle lightly with confectioners' sugar. Serve with strawberry coulis.

Yields 12 servings

126

Orange Yogurt Cream

1 quart nonfat vanilla yogurt

1 tablespoon unsweetened frozen orange
   juice concentrate

1 tablespoon Grand Marnier

1 tablespoon granulated fructose

1 tablespoon orange zest

nutrition per serving

CAL	CARB	PRO	FAT	FIBER	CHOL	SOD
81	16g	4g	<1g	<1g	1mg	56mg

1 Combine the yogurt, orange juice concentrate, Grand Marnier, fructose and orange zest in a small bowl and whisk until blended.

2 Chill, covered, until ready to serve.

Yields 12 servings

Heirloom Tomato Hummus

1 Combine the undrained garbanzo beans, garlic, coriander, cumin, paprika, black pepper, white pepper, cayenne pepper and kosher salt in a saucepan and mix well. Simmer until most of the liquid has evaporated. Remove to a food processor and process until smooth, scraping the side of the processor with a spatula.

2 Add the stock, tahini, olive oil and lemon juice and process until smooth. Adjust the seasonings and add the tomato. Process for 20 seconds. Spoon into a bowl and chill for 2 hours. Serve with warm bread, pita or chips.

3 For a sweet finish to hummus, add chopped fresh basil at the end.

Yields 6 servings

1 (16-ounce) can garbanzo beans

3 garlic cloves

1 tablespoon each coriander and cumin

1/2 tablespoon paprika

1/2 teaspoon black pepper

1/4 teaspoon white pepper

1/4 teaspoon cayenne pepper

2 teaspoons kosher salt

1/4 cup chicken stock or vegetable stock

1 teaspoon tahini (sesame paste)

1 teaspoon extra-virgin olive oil

juice of 2 lemons

2 heirloom tomatoes, chopped

nutrition per serving

CAL	CARB	PRO	FAT	FIBER	CHOL	SOD
94	14g	4g	2g	4g	<1mg	887mg

Corn Chowder

1 Combine the corn ears and potato with the milk and the stock in a saucepan. Cook for 10 to 12 minutes or until the potatoes are tender. Remove the corn from the saucepan and let cool. Cut the kernels from the ears.

2 Sauté the bell pepper, celery, onion, carrot and garlic in the olive oil in a saucepan until tender. Stir in the corn and flour. Add to the milk and potato mixture and stir in the coconut milk.

3 Bring to a boil, stirring constantly. Reduce the heat and simmer for 5 minutes, stirring constantly. Stir in the cilantro and serve.

4 You may substitute low-fat milk for the coconut milk. For a dairy-free soup, substitute chicken stock or vegetable stock for the 4 cups milk, add plain soy milk, and purée half the soup.

Yields 8 servings

6 ears corn on the cob, roasted

1 potato, peeled and chopped

4 cups nonfat milk

3 cups vegetable stock or chicken stock

1 red bell pepper, chopped

3 ribs celery, chopped

1 onion, chopped

1 carrot, chopped

3 garlic cloves

1 tablespoon olive oil

2 tablespoons flour

1/2 cup light coconut milk (optional)

2 tablespoons chopped fresh cilantro

week two thursday

nutrition per serving

CAL	CARB	PRO	FAT	FIBER	CHOL	SOD
139	26g	6g	3g	4g	2mg	77mg

Grilled Duck with Caramelized Figs

1 pound boneless skinless lean
   duck breasts

1/2 cup minced red onion

14 dried or fresh figs, cut into quarters

1/4 cup orange juice

1/4 cup white wine

2 large shallots, chopped

1 tablespoon minced garlic

1 teaspoon olive oil

1/2 cup marsala

2 tablespoons balsamic vinegar

3 cups chicken stock

1/4 teaspoon cardamom

1/8 teaspoon cumin

1/8 teaspoon ground cinnamon

1 teaspoon arrowroot or cornstarch

3 Yukon Gold potatoes

chopped parsley to taste

8 cups baby vegetables

parsley sprigs, for garnish

1   Grill the duck breasts until partially cooked through. Preheat the oven to 500 degrees and place the duck on a roasting pan; set aside.

2   Sauté the onion in a sauté pan sprayed with olive oil cooking spray. Add 10 of the figs, orange juice and white wine. Simmer for about 10 minutes; keep warm.

3   Sauté the shallots and garlic in 1 teaspoon olive oil in a sauté pan. Add the marsala and balsamic vinegar, stirring to deglaze the pan. Cook until the liquid has nearly evaporated. Add the stock, the remaining 4 figs, cardamom, cumin and cinnamon.

4   Bring to a low boil and cook until reduced to 1 1/2 to 2 cups. Process in a blender until smooth. Blend the arrowroot with a small amount of cold water and add to the sauce. Cook until thickened, stirring constantly; keep warm.

5   Cook the potatoes in enough water to cover until tender. Drain and peel the potatoes and toss with chopped parsley in a bowl. Steam the baby vegetables until tender-crisp. Keep the potatoes and vegetables warm.

6   Roast the duck in the oven for 12 to 15 minutes or until cooked through. Place 2 ounces duck on each of 8 serving plates. Spoon 1 ounce of the sauce over the top. Arrange the potatoes and steamed vegetables around the duck and finish with the caramelized figs and fresh parsley.

Yields 8 servings

nutrition per serving

CAL	CARB	PRO	FAT	FIBER	CHOL	SOD
230	28g	20g	4g	6g	58mg	143mg

Piña Colada Sorbet

1 Combine the sugar, Splenda, orange juice and water in a saucepan and mix well. Bring to a boil and remove from the heat.

2 Process the pineapple with the coconut milk in a blender until puréed. Add the rum and orange juice mixture and process until smooth. Spoon into a freezer-safe container and freeze until firm.

3 Scrape the frozen mixture with an ice cream scoop and place in serving bowls. Garnish with toasted shredded coconut.

Yields 6 servings

¹/4 cup sugar

¹/2 cup Splenda

¹/2 cup orange juice

¹/2 cup water

1 ripe pineapple, chopped

¹/2 light coconut milk

2 tablespoons rum

toasted shredded coconut, for garnish

nutrition per serving						
CAL	CARB	PRO	FAT	FIBER	CHOL	SOD
116	23g	1g	1g	1g	0mg	1mg

friday menu

breakfast

Asparagus Fontina Yogurt Soufflé

lunch

House-Smoked Salmon with Asian Cucumber Salad
Spearmint and Pear Granita with Mixed Fruit

hors d'oeuvre

Turkey Basil Meatballs

dinner

Strawberry and Goat Cheese Spinach Salad
with Balsamic Vinaigrette
Hoisin-Crusted Shrimp
Thai Curry Sauce
Sweet Potato Mash
Stir-Fried Vegetables

dessert

Mocha Mousse

Asparagus Fontina Yogurt Soufflé

1 Preheat the oven to 325 degrees. Spray four 1-cup soufflé dishes with butter-flavor nonstick cooking spray. Combine the asparagus, yogurt, egg yolk, parsley and 2 tablespoons of the cheese in a food processor; process until puréed. Remove to a medium bowl.

2 Beat the egg whites in a bowl until foamy. Add the cornstarch and salt, beating constantly until the egg whites are stiff and glossy. Fold $1/3$ of the egg whites into the asparagus mixture, then fold in the remaining egg whites.

3 Spoon into the prepared soufflé dishes and sprinkle with the remaining 1 tablespoon cheese. Bake for 30 to 40 minutes or until set.

Yields 4 servings

$1/2$ **cup chopped cooked asparagus**

$1/3$ **cup low-fat vanilla yogurt**

1 egg yolk

2 tablespoons chopped parsley

3 tablespoons grated fontina cheese or Parmesan cheese

2 egg whites

1 tablespoon cornstarch or arrowroot

$1/4$ **teaspoon salt**

nutrition per serving						
CAL	CARB	PRO	FAT	FIBER	CHOL	SOD
69	7g	4g	3g	1g	58mg	206mg

131

House-Smoked Salmon with Asian Cucumber Salad

Sesame Vinaigrette

1/4 cup rice vinegar

1 teaspoon olive oil

1 teaspoon sesame oil

sea salt to taste

Salmon and Salad

6 (3-ounce) fresh salmon fillets

1/4 cup fresh lemon juice

salt and pepper to taste

6 cups mixed baby greens

2 hothouse cucumbers, julienned

1 large carrot, julienned

6 to 10 basil leaves, julienned

18 cherry tomatoes, for garnish

6 chervil sprigs, for garnish

12 stone-ground whole wheat crackers

1   For the vinaigrette, combine the vinegar, olive oil, sesame oil and sea salt in a bowl and mix well.

2   For the salmon and salad, heat a smoker to medium to medium-hot. Sprinkle the salmon fillets with the lemon juice and season with salt and pepper. Smoke the salmon until cooked through.

3   Combine the mixed greens with the cucumbers, carrot and basil leaves in a bowl. Add the vinaigrette and toss to mix well. Spoon onto serving plates and top with the salmon. Garnish each plate with 3 cherry tomatoes and a chervil sprig. Serve with 2 stone-ground whole wheat crackers.

Yields 6 servings

nutrition per serving						
CAL	CARB	PRO	FAT	FIBER	CHOL	SOD
285	19g	27g	11g	3g	74mg	134mg

Spearmint and Pear Granita with Mixed Fruit

7 ounces pear purée

1 cup water

1/2 cup sugar

1 tablespoon lemon juice

4 sprigs fresh spearmint

4 cantaloupe balls

8 strawberries

8 pineapple tidbits

1 kumquat, thinly sliced

4 sprigs of mint, for garnish

4 strawberries drizzled with
   white chocolate (optional)

nutrition per serving

CAL	CARB	PRO	FAT	FIBER	CHOL	SOD
174	41g	1g	2g	2g	<1mg	9mg

1 Chill a 9×13-inch nonreactive metal pan in the freezer. Combine the pear purée, water, sugar, lemon juice and spearmint sprigs in a saucepan. Cook over medium heat until the sugar dissolves, stirring constantly. Pour into a medium bowl and place in a larger bowl of ice water. Let stand until cool, stirring frequently.

2 Pour into the chilled pan; remove and discard the spearmint sprigs. Freeze for 1 hour or until the mixture is icy around the edges. Break up the icy edges with a large spoon and stir toward the center. Freeze for 2 hours longer, stirring again after 1 hour.

3 Combine the cantaloupe, strawberries, pineapple and kumquat in a bowl. Chill in the refrigerator. Scrape the frozen mixture into large crystals with a fork and spoon into chilled wine glasses. Top with the mixed fruit. Garnish each serving with a sprig of mint and a strawberry drizzled with white chocolate.

Yields 4 servings

You can substitute other meats for the turkey in this recipe, but you must remember that you will also add more fat. You can also change the herbs and spices to give it an ethnic twist. We like to serve a spicy marinara dipping sauce with it.

Turkey Basil Meatballs

1 tablespoon extra-virgin olive oil

1 red onion, minced

2 tablespoons minced garlic

1 pound finely ground (95% fat-free) turkey

1/4 cup tightly packed chopped fresh basil

1/4 cup panko (Japanese bread crumbs)

1 egg

1 egg white

2 tablespoons Worcestershire sauce

2 tablespoons grated Parmesan cheese

salt and pepper to taste

1 Heat the olive oil in a small sauté pan over low heat. Add the onion and garlic and sauté for 5 minutes or until tender but not brown. Cool for 5 minutes.

2 Combine with the turkey, basil, panko, egg, egg white, Worcestershire sauce, cheese, salt and pepper in a medium bowl. Chill in the refrigerator for 20 to 30 minutes.

3 Preheat the oven to 450 degrees. Shape the turkey mixture into balls by hand or with a small ice cream scoop. Arrange 1 inch apart on a baking sheet. Bake for 10 to 12 minutes or until firm and cooked through, turning once to brown evenly. Serve hot with cocktail forks or wooden picks.

Yields 40 meatballs

nutrition per meatball						
CAL	CARB	PRO	FAT	FIBER	CHOL	SOD
27	1g	2g	1g	<1g	14mg	31mg

There are many different kinds of goat cheese, also known as chèvre. There are good domestic goat cheeses from Wisconsin. We prefer a moderately-priced balsamic vinegar from Modena because it is good with berries. You can serve this salad with salmon or other fish entrées in place of a starch.

Spinach Salad with Strawberries and Goat Cheese

1 Combine the spinach with the Balsamic Vinaigrette in a bowl and toss to coat evenly. Season with salt and pepper and mix in the strawberries gently.

2 Spoon onto chilled plates and sprinkle with the goat cheese.

Yields 5 servings

4 cups baby spinach

1/2 cup Balsamic Vinaigrette (below)

salt and pepper to taste

1 cup strawberries, sliced

3 ounces goat cheese, crumbled

nutrition per serving

CAL	CARB	PRO	FAT	FIBER	CHOL	SOD
81	5g	4g	5g	2g	13mg	119mg

Balsamic Vinaigrette

1 Combine the olive oil, vinegar, ice water, shallot, Dijon mustard, thyme, xanthan gum, salt and pepper in a blender.

2 Process at high speed for 30 seconds or until smooth. Store in the refrigerator.

Yields 2 1/2 cups

2 tablespoons extra-virgin olive oil

1/3 cup balsamic vinegar

2 cups ice water

1 large shallot

1 teaspoon Dijon mustard

1 tablespoon chopped fresh thyme

1/2 teaspoon xanthan gum

salt and pepper to taste

nutrition per serving

CAL	CARB	PRO	FAT	FIBER	CHOL	SOD
18	2g	<1g	1g	<1g	0mg	14mg

To keep shrimp plump and moist, take care not to overcook them. You can substitute yams for the sweet potatoes in the mash or mix the two. Sweet potatoes are the best complex carbohydrate you can find, so don't be fooled into thinking they are bad for you because of their sweetness. The Thai Curry Sauce is optional, for sometimes the shrimp and creamy sweet potatoes are just the right combination without it.

Hoisin-Crusted Shrimp

1 pound (16- to 20-count) shrimp

2 tablespoons hoisin sauce

1 tablespoon light soy sauce

1 tablespoon sesame oil

1 teaspoon sherry

1 teaspoon sambal (chili sauce)

1 teaspoon Madras curry powder

1 teaspoon granulated onion

1 teaspoon granulated garlic

1 teaspoon ginger

1 tablespoon peanut oil

1   Peel and devein the shrimp, reserving the shells for the Thai Curry Sauce. Combine the hoisin sauce, soy sauce, sesame oil, sherry, sambal, curry powder, granulated onion, granulated garlic and ginger in a bowl and mix well. Add the shrimp and mix well. Marinate in the refrigerator for 4 hours.

2   Heat the peanut oil until smoking in a nonstick sauté pan. Add the shrimp in a single layer, taking care not to overcrowd. Sauté for 1 minute on each side or until pink and cooked through, turning once.

3   You can finish the shrimp in a 450-degree oven for 2 to 3 minutes if not done to taste, but do not overcook, as they will become tough. Serve with Sweet Potato Mash (page 137) and Thai Curry Sauce (page 137).

Yields 6 servings

nutrition per serving

CAL	CARB	PRO	FAT	FIBER	CHOL	SOD
77	4g	4g	5g	<1g	27mg	238mg

week two friday

Thai Curry Sauce

1   Heat the oil to smoking in a medium saucepan over high heat. Add the shrimp shells and sauté for 3 to 5 minutes or until red. Add the carrot, onion, celery, lemon grass, garlic and ginger. Reduce the heat to medium-low to low and stir in the coconut milk. Cook for about 5 minutes or until the vegetables are tender.

2   Stir in the tomato paste and curry paste. Add the wine and cook until most of it has evaporated. Add filtered water just to the level of the shells. Simmer for 1 hour. Pour the mixture, with the shells, into a blender in batches, filling the blender only halfway. Process for 1 minute or until smooth.

3   Strain the batches into a saucepan and stir in a slurry of the cornstarch and warm water. Season with salt and white pepper and cook until thickened, stirring constantly.

Yields 6 servings

2 tablespoons vegetable oil

4 cups uncooked shrimp shells (from the Hoisin-Crusted Shrimp)

1/4 cup finely chopped carrot

1/4 cup finely chopped onion

1/4 cup finely chopped celery

2 tablespoons chopped lemon grass

2 tablespoons chopped garlic

2 tablespoons chopped fresh ginger

1/2 small can light coconut milk

3 tablespoons tomato paste

1 tablespoon Thai red curry paste

1/4 cup dry white wine

2 tablespoons cornstarch

2 tablespoons warm water

salt and white pepper to taste

nutrition per serving						
CAL	CARB	PRO	FAT	FIBER	CHOL	SOD
103	8g	1g	7g	1g	0mg	81mg

Sweet Potato Mash

1   Preheat the oven to 400 degrees. Pierce the sweet potatoes several times with a sharp knife to release steam. Wrap tightly in foil and place on a baking sheet. Bake for 1 to 1 1/2 hours or until very tender. Cool at room temperature for 30 minutes or longer.

2   Peel the sweet potatoes and combine with the coconut milk, almond oil, salt and pepper in a bowl. Beat with a whisk attachment or mix with a whisk until light and fluffy.

Yields 6 servings

2 sweet potatoes

1/4 cup light coconut milk

1 teaspoon almond oil

salt and pepper to taste

nutrition per serving						
CAL	CARB	PRO	FAT	FIBER	CHOL	SOD
101	21g	1g	2g	3g	0mg	8mg

week two friday

Stir-Fried Vegetables

4 cups julienned napa cabbage

1 cup julienned snow peas

1/2 cup julienned red onion

1 carrot, julienned

2 cups bean sprouts

1 cup broccoli florets

1 bunch scallions, cut into 1/2-inch pieces

1 tablespoon cornstarch

1 tablespoon peanut oil

1 teaspoon grated fresh ginger

1 teaspoon minced garlic

2 teaspoons Splenda

1/4 cup light soy sauce

1/4 cup mirin (sweet rice wine)

salt and pepper to taste

1   Combine the cabbage, snow peas, onion and carrot in a bowl. Add the bean sprouts, broccoli florets and scallions. Toss with the cornstarch, coating evenly.

2   Heat the peanut oil to smoking in a large nonstick sauté pan. Add the vegetable mixture and stir-fry for about 3 minutes or until tender-crisp. Add the ginger and garlic and stir-fry lightly. Stir in the Splenda, soy sauce, mirin, salt and pepper.

3   You can add a small amount of chicken broth if needed to reach the desired consistency. Do not overcook, as the vegetables should still be colorful and crunchy.

Yields 6 servings

138

nutrition per serving

CAL	CARB	PRO	FAT	FIBER	CHOL	SOD
93	14g	3g	3g	3g	0mg	621mg

Mocha Mousse

2 tablespoon Kahlúa

1 tablespoon instant coffee granules

2 (12-ounce) packages of light extra-firm silken tofu

1/2 cup baking cocoa

1/2 cup pure maple syrup

1 tablespoon vanilla extract

1 teaspoon ground cinnamon

1   Heat the Kahlúa in a small saucepan. Add the coffee granules and stir to dissolve completely. Combine the tofu with the baking cocoa, maple syrup, vanilla and cinnamon in a food processor fitted with a metal blade.

2   Add the coffee mixture and process for 7 to 10 minutes or until thickened and smooth. Spoon into a bowl and chill for 20 minutes or longer. Garnish with raspberries and fresh mint.

3   For a nice presentation, alternate layers of the mousse with freshly whipped cream in wine glasses.

Yields 6 servings

nutrition per serving

CAL	CARB	PRO	FAT	FIBER	CHOL	SOD
149	26g	9g	2g	2g	0mg	104mg

saturday menu
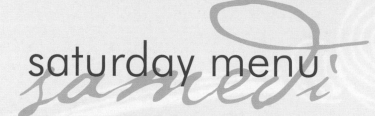

breakfast

Maple Walnut Oatmeal

lunch

Spring Mix with Creamy Black Pepper Dressing

Barbecued Chicken Pizza

Raspberry Meringue Cups

hors d'oeuvre

Ahi Tuna Tartare with Baked Sweet Potato Chips

dinner

Roasted Butternut Squash Soup with Cinnamon

Kalamata Olive-Crusted Colorado Lamb

Cal-a-Vie Ratatouille

Celery Root Purée

dessert

Blueberry Streusel Cake

Maple Walnut Oatmeal

1 Bring the milk to a boil in a saucepan. Stir in the oats and return to a boil. Reduce the heat and simmer for 5 minutes.

2 Add the maple syrup, brown sugar, walnuts, currants, vanilla, cinnamon and salt to taste and mix well. Cook until tender and smooth. Serve hot, and garnish each serving with a sliced strawberry.

Yields 6 servings

5 cups nonfat milk, or 2 cups milk and
  3 cups water

2 cups rolled oats

1/4 cup maple syrup

1 tablespoon brown sugar

1/2 cup toasted chopped walnuts

1/2 cup currants or raisins (optional)

1 teaspoon vanilla extract

1 teaspoon ground cinnamon

6 strawberries, for garnish

nutrition per serving						
CAL	CARB	PRO	FAT	FIBER	CHOL	SOD
326	51g	13g	9g	5g	4mg	210mg

Spring Mix with Creamy Black Pepper Dressing

1 For the dressing, combine the shallot, garlic, yogurt, mustard, lemon juice, vinegar, honey, olive oil, pepper and salt in a blender; process until creamy. You may substitute skim buttermilk for the yogurt.

2 For the salad, combine the lettuce, cucumber and tomatoes in a bowl. Add the dressing and toss to coat evenly.

Yield 8 servings

Dressing

1 shallot

1 garlic clove

1/2 cup nonfat plain yogurt

2 tablespoons each whole grain mustard,
  lemon juice and sherry wine vinegar

1 tablespoon honey

1 tablespoon olive oil

1/2 teaspoon pepper

1/2 teaspoon salt (optional)

Salad

8 cups spring mix lettuce

1 cucumber, diced

32 cherry tomatoes

nutrition per serving						
CAL	CARB	PRO	FAT	FIBER	CHOL	SOD
35	4g	1g	2g	<1g	<1mg	192mg

week two saturday

For a crisp pizza, roll the dough thin. About two minutes before the pizza finishes baking, place on a pizza stone on the bottom rack of the oven.

Barbecued Chicken Pizza

Pizza Crust

2 tablespoons dry yeast

1¹/2 cups warm water

2 tablespoons sugar or Splenda

1 tablespoon olive oil

salt to taste

2¹/2 cups unbleached flour

2¹/2 cups whole wheat pastry flour

Pizza

6 (4-ounce) chicken breasts, cooked and
    finely chopped

1 cup thinly sliced scallions

1/2 cup chopped fresh cilantro

3 cups barbecue sauce

1¹/2 cups (6 ounces) shredded
    mozzarella cheese

1/2 cup (2 ounces) grated Parmesan cheese

1   For the crust, combine the yeast, water, sugar, olive oil and salt in a bowl and let stand until foamy. Add the unbleached flour and whole wheat flour and mix to form a firm dough. Knead well on a lightly floured surface. Place in a lightly oiled bowl, turning to coat the surface. Cover with a towel and let rise for 30 minutes or until doubled in bulk.

2   Spray three 12-inch pizza pans lightly with olive oil cooking spray and sprinkle with cornmeal. Roll the dough on a lightly floured surface and fit into the pans. Cover with plastic wrap and refrigerate until needed.

3   For the pizza, preheat the oven to 500 degrees. Combine the chicken, scallions and cilantro with 1 cup of the barbecue sauce in a bowl and toss to mix well. Spread the remaining 2 cups barbecue sauce over the pizza dough. Layer the chicken mixture over the sauce and top with the mozzarella and Parmesan cheeses. Bake for about 20 minutes or until golden brown.

4   Nutritional analysis includes the pizza crust.

Yields 12 servings

nutrition per serving						
CAL	CARB	PRO	FAT	FIBER	CHOL	SOD
466	62g	29g	11g	4g	54mg	844mg

Raspberry Meringue Cups

Raspberry Purée

2 cups fresh raspberries

1 tablespoon honey

1/3 cup fresh orange juice (about 1 orange)

Meringue Cups

6 egg whites, at room temperature

1/4 teaspoon salt

1 cup sugar

1 teaspoon vanilla extract

Berry Filling

3 cups mixed berries, such as raspberries,
   blueberries, strawberries and
   blackberries

3 tablespoons Chambord or amaretto
   (optional)

confectioners' sugar and fresh mint sprigs,
   for garnish

1 For the purée, combine the raspberries, honey and orange juice in a blender or food processor. Process until smooth and strain into a bowl.

2 For the meringue cups, preheat the oven to 225 degrees. Beat the egg whites with the salt in a bowl until foamy. Add the sugar 1 tablespoon at a time, beating constantly until the mixture is smooth and the sugar dissolves completely. Add the vanilla and 2 tablespoons of the raspberry purée, beating constantly until stiff peaks form.

3 Spoon the meringue mixture into a pastry bag fitted with a star tip. Pipe into cups on a parchment-lined baking sheet, beginning at the center point and working in a spiral until the cups measure 3 inches in diameter and 1 1/2 inches in height.

4 Bake the cups for 1 hour. Turn off the oven and let the cups stand in the oven until completely cool and dry.

5 For the filling, combine the berries with the remaining raspberry purée and the liqueur in a bowl. Spoon into the meringue cups and garnish with confectioners' sugar and mint sprigs.

Yields 8 servings

nutrition per serving						
CAL	CARB	PRO	FAT	FIBER	CHOL	SOD
186	41g	3g	<1g	3g	0mg	110mg

To make baked sweet potato chips, peel one sweet potato and slice it very thin on a mandoline. Place in a small bowl and spray generously with nonstick cooking spray. Season with salt and white pepper. Spread in a single layer on a baking sheet sprayed with nonstick cooking spray. Bake at 375 degrees for 25 to 30 minutes or until crisp and golden brown. Cool to room temperature.

Ahi Tuna Tartare with Baked Sweet Potato Chips

1 Combine the mayonnaise, shallot, ginger and wasabi in a small bowl. Whisk in the soy sauce, vinegar and mirin. Add the sesame oil gradually, whisking constantly to emulsify.

2 Place the tuna in a bowl and add enough of the mayonnaise mixture to bind, mixing well. Cover directly with plastic wrap and chill in the refrigerator for up to 48 hours.

3 Spoon 1/2 tablespoon onto Baked Sweet Potato Chips (above) or your favorite flavor Terra Chips.

Yields 20 servings

1 tablespoon fat-free mayonnaise

1 large shallot, finely chopped

1/2 teaspoon grated peeled fresh ginger

1/2 teaspoon dry fat-free wasabi
   (Japanese horseradish)

2 teaspoons light soy sauce

2 teaspoons unseasoned rice vinegar

2 teaspoons mirin (sweet rice wine)

1 teaspoon sesame oil

8 ounces sushi-grade ahi tuna,
   finely chopped

145

nutrition per serving						
CAL	CARB	PRO	FAT	FIBER	CHOL	SOD
18	<1g	3g	1g	<1g	6mg	37mg

week two saturday

Butternut squash is one of our favorite fall squashes. It is interchangeable with the kabocha or the sweet pie pumpkin when butternut is not available. You can rinse and dry the seeds and toast them like pumpkin seeds. Spray them with nonstick cooking spray, sprinkle with salt, spread evenly on a baking sheet, and toast at 350 degrees until dry.

Roasted Butternut Squash with Cinnamon

1 butternut squash

1 teaspoon vegetable oil

1/2 teaspoon ground cinnamon

1/2 cup finely chopped yellow onion

4 cups (or more) chicken stock or
  vegetable stock

salt and white pepper to taste

1/2 cup light coconut milk

nutrition per serving

CAL	CARB	PRO	FAT	FIBER	CHOL	SOD
79	13g	3g	2g	2g	2mg	131mg

1 Preheat the oven to 400 degrees. Peel the squash and cut into 1/2-inch pieces, discarding the seeds. Combine with the oil and cinnamon in a bowl and mix well. Spread on a baking sheet and roast for 20 to 30 minutes or until medium brown.

2 Spray a medium saucepan with nonstick cooking spray for 3 seconds. Add the onion and sauté over low heat for 3 to 4 minutes or until the onion is tender. Add the squash and mix well. Increase the heat and add enough stock to cover the vegetables by 1 inch. Season with salt and white pepper.

3 Bring to a boil and reduce the heat. Simmer for 15 to 20 minutes or until done to taste, adding additional stock if needed for the desired consistency. Add the coconut milk. Process the mixture in a blender at high speed for 30 seconds or until smooth. Adjust the seasonings and serve hot.

Yields 12 servings

146

week two saturday

The final dinner at Cal-a-Vie is usually the most memorable one, and this is no exception. We recommend Colorado lamb because of its thickness and full flavor. Be sure to let it stand for five minutes before slicing to preserve all the natural juices. The most important tip is to season the lamb with salt and pepper before cooking and brush it with mustard so the olive crust will stick properly.

Kalamata Olive-Crusted Colorado Lamb

1 Preheat the oven to 450 degrees. Process the olives with the garlic, rosemary, thyme, 1/2 teaspoon pepper and the olive oil in a food processor until chunky. Add just enough water to make a paste, processing constantly.

2 Season the lamb with salt and pepper. Sear on both sides in a large ovenproof sauté pan sprayed with nonstick cooking spray. Use a pastry brush to coat the lamb immediately with the Dijon mustard and then press the olive paste evenly over the lamb.

3 Return the lamb to the sauté pan. Roast for 20 to 25 minutes or to an internal temperature of 125 to 135 degrees. Let stand for 5 minutes before slicing to serve.

Yields 5 servings

1/4 cup kalamata olives

1 garlic clove

1 teaspoon fresh rosemary

1 teaspoon fresh thyme

1/2 teaspoon pepper

1 teaspoon extra-virgin olive oil

2 (7-bone) racks Colorado lamb, trimmed
    and frenched

salt and pepper to taste

2 tablespoons Dijon mustard

nutrition per serving						
CAL	CARB	PRO	FAT	FIBER	CHOL	SOD
171	2g	18g	10g	<1g	56mg	350mg

week two saturday

Cal-a-Vie Ratatouille

1 eggplant

1/2 small red onion

1 red bell pepper

1 yellow bell pepper

1 orange bell pepper (optional)

1 large zucchini

1 large yellow squash

2 tablespoons (or more) pomace olive oil

salt and pepper to taste

1 tablespoon crushed garlic

1 tablespoon chopped fresh rosemary

1 teaspoon chopped fresh thyme

3 Roma tomatoes, chopped

1 Rinse the eggplant, onion, bell peppers, zucchini and squash with cold water. Cut off the end of the vegetables and square them to dice evenly. Cut into even pieces, keeping each vegetable separate.

2 Heat the olive oil to warm in a large stockpot. Add the eggplant and sauté just until tender. Season with salt and pepper. Add the remaining vegetables in the order listed, sautéing each just until tender. Sprinkle with salt and additional olive oil or spray with nonstick cooking spray if the mixture appears dry.

3 Add the garlic, rosemary, thyme and tomatoes and sauté just until the tomatoes are tender. Season with salt and pepper.

Yields 6 servings

nutrition per serving						
CAL	CARB	PRO	FAT	FIBER	CHOL	SOD
88	11g	2g	5g	3g	0mg	7mg

Celery Root Purée

2 cups peeled and chopped celery root

1 tablespoon salt

1 tablespoon almond oil

1/4 cup light coconut milk

salt and pepper to taste

1 Combine the celery root with 1 tablespoon salt and enough water to cover in a saucepan. Bring to a boil and reduce the heat. Simmer until tender and drain.

2 Process in a food processor until puréed. Add the almond oil and coconut milk and mix well. Season with salt and pepper and serve hot.

Yields 4 servings

nutrition per serving						
CAL	CARB	PRO	FAT	FIBER	CHOL	SOD
63	5g	1g	5g	1g	0mg	47mg

Blueberry Streusel Cake

1 Preheat the oven to 350 degrees. Combine the blueberries with $^1/_4$ cup sugar in a bowl and crush gently with a potato masher. Let stand for 5 minutes or longer. Mix the cookie crumbs, brown sugar, butter and orange juice in a bowl.

2 Combine the unbleached flour, whole wheat flour, $^1/_3$ cup sugar, the baking powder, baking soda and salt in a large bowl. Combine the yogurt, almond oil, egg, egg white, orange zest and vanilla in a medium bowl and whisk to mix well. Add to the flour mixture and stir to mix well. Fold in the blueberries.

3 Spoon into a 9-inch cake pan sprayed with nonstick cooking spray. Bake for 30 minutes. Sprinkle the cookie crumb mixture evenly over the top. Bake for 10 minutes longer or until a wooden pick inserted in the center comes out clean. Remove to a wire rack to cool.

Yields 16 servings

1 $^1/_2$ cups blueberries

$^1/_4$ cup sugar

$^1/_3$ cup amaretti cookie crumbs

$^1/_4$ cup packed brown sugar

1 tablespoon butter, melted

1 teaspoon orange juice

$^3/_4$ cup unbleached flour

$^3/_4$ cup whole wheat pastry flour

$^1/_3$ cup sugar

$^3/_4$ teaspoon baking powder

$^1/_4$ teaspoon baking soda

$^1/_8$ teaspoon salt

$^3/_4$ cup nonfat vanilla yogurt

2 tablespoons almond oil

1 egg

1 egg white

1 tablespoon grated orange zest

1 teaspoon vanilla extract

149

nutrition per serving						
CAL	CARB	PRO	FAT	FIBER	CHOL	SOD
135	24g	3g	3g	1g	15mg	93mg

week two saturday

guests' favorites

The ultimate haven of health, Cal-a-Vie is about much more than pampering. A combination of physical activities tailored to your fitness goals and relaxing spa treatments enriches and invigorates you, making Cal-a-Vie the ultimate spa experience.

Cal-a-Vie's fitness program is a comprehensive regimen designed to help you achieve personal fitness goals, such as stress reduction, relaxation, and weight control. A personal fitness assessment is used to develop a sensible, integrated, and balanced program of exercise and nutrition—one that will fit into your lifestyle to produce lasting results. Whether you are just getting started in exercise, or are at a high level of fitness, there is something here for you.

Cal-a-Vie's advanced therapy program was developed in coordination with international health and beauty experts. Beauty and skin care treatments for men and women help to cleanse and invigorate your body. Cal-a-Vie offers a therapy program unlike any other in the country, utilizing sophisticated European techniques of thalassotherapy, hydrotherapy, and aromatherapy. These sensible therapeutic treatments help restore your body to its natural balance. You will feel relaxed, content, and deliciously pampered as inner serenity returns.

keeping your balance at the table

The first key in finding balance at the table is to take in the recommended daily amount of calories. For most sedentary adults, the approximate number of calories can be calculated by multiplying current body weight by twelve. This calculation will vary if one exercises or wants to lose or gain weight.

Become familiar with how many calories you take in on a given day. This number should align with the number of calories your body actually requires to maintain an ideal body weight. Calorie-dense foods that add up quickly are cakes, candy, chocolate, foods high in fat, and beverages (870 calories in a coconut crème frappuccino). These foods can be enjoyable, but the key is balance. Read and understand ingredient and serving size labels.

A second key in finding your food balance is to remember portion control. The body has a much easier time digesting smaller meals. Asking the system to work in overdrive all the time breaks down the body's digestive machinery just like any other overworked body part or organ.

Eating calorie-controlled meals throughout the day takes a scheduled effort. Meals should be planned and times should be fairly regular. Try to eat four to six times a day. If you find yourself hungry, prepare a healthy snack, don't just grab whatever is quick and easy. Extreme hunger encourages overeating.

A third key in finding your food balance is to consider the actual food choices you are making. Although research is continually being conducted and lists change from day to day, some of the Best and Worst Food Choices are listed below:

Best Food Choices

Broccoli: rich source of fiber, vitamins A and C, folic acid, calcium, and magnesium

Berries: full of fiber, minerals, vitamins, and antioxidants

Tomatoes: excellent source of vitamin C, lycopene, and linked in studies showing significantly lower rates of prostate cancer in men that consumed tomatoes

Yams/Sweet potatoes: loaded with carotenoids, vitamin C, potassium, and fiber

Whole grains: emphasis on **whole** grains, potent source of phytochemiclas, vitamin E, and phytic acid (IP-6), a powerful antioxidant

Eggs/egg whites: back on the list, with other protein sources way down on the list because of saturated fat, hormone, antibiotic, and mercury levels—although eggs/egg whites should be from cage-free chickens fed only natural products

Worst Food Choices

Soda: full of sugars and/or artificial sweeteners

Partially hydrogenated oils: found in most baked products, almost every packaged cookie, chip and cracker

Artificial flavors, colors, MSG: additives that do no favors for the body systems

Granola/granola bars: mostly sugars and refined grains, some candy bars are more nutrient dense

Saturated fats: fats from animals, found in meats, whole milk, cheese and cream

High fructose corn syrup: a common and affordable sweetener, empty calories that stimulate insulin production in the body

The most important advice for shopping for food is to read product labels. The ingredients on a product are listed in descending order, from those present in the greatest amount to those present in the least. Avoid products whose list is long and those filled with many unrecognizable ingredients. Compare the food label to what you could make at home. If the ingredients in the product are vastly different from what you would prepare in your kitchen, avoid the food item. Finally, look for unhealthy ingredients, such as partially hydrogenated oils and artificial colors.

If the product passes these "tests," check the nutrition labeling. Start by looking at calories per serving and what a serving size is. A bag of trail mix may actually "serve 6," and if you eat the whole bag, you must multiply all numbers by 6. Consider the breakdown of nutrients and the percentages of fat, calories, and protein. Note what kinds of fat are in the product, the sodium level, and cholesterol content.

Some basic rules to follow:

1. Check the serving size and main nutrients; analyze if this is what you really wish to consume.

2. Avoid products that have many unfamiliar ingredients or lots of additives and unfamiliar ingredients.

3. Buy foods that are similar to what you would prepare/use at home.

4. Avoid partially hydrogenated oils, artificial colors, artificial sweeteners, nitrites, or nitrates, sulfites, potassium bromate, and brominated vegetable oil. All of these pose health risks if consumed regularly.

5. Minimize consumption of products containing MSG, aluminum, and preservatives BHA, BHT, and TBHQ. These are also associated with increased health risks.

6. Look for products as close to the natural source as possible—think plant sources, whole grains, fresh fruits, and vegetables.

Shrimp Spring Rolls with Sweet-and-Sour Dipping Sauce

Sweet-and-Sour Dipping Sauce

1/2 cup unseasoned rice vinegar

1/2 cup mirin (sweet rice wine)

1/4 cup sugar or Splenda

2 tablespoons light soy sauce

1 teaspoon fish sauce

1/2 teaspoon sambal (chili sauce)

1 tablespoon chopped cilantro

1/2 teaspoon grated fresh ginger

nutrition per serving						
CAL	CARB	PRO	FAT	FIBER	CHOL	SOD
16	3g	<1g	0g	<1g	0mg	71mg

Shrimp Spring Rolls

1 pound shrimp, peeled and deveined

1 1/2 quarts water

1/2 cup dry white wine

1 small onion, chopped

juice of 1 lemon

2 bay leaves

1 teaspoon salt

8 black peppercorns

1/4 cup honey

2 teaspoons sambal (chili sauce)

8 (10-inch) sheets rice paper

baby lettuce

1 mango, sliced into strips

1 bunch mint leaves

1 bunch basil leaves

nutrition per serving						
CAL	CARB	PRO	FAT	FIBER	CHOL	SOD
30	4g	3g	<1g	<1g	22mg	34mg

1 For the dipping sauce, combine the vinegar, mirin and sugar in a saucepan and bring to a boil. Remove from the heat and cool. Combine with the soy sauce, fish sauce, sambal, cilantro and ginger in a bowl and whisk to mix well. Chill until serving time.

2 For the shrimp spring rolls, combine the shrimp with the water, wine, onion, lemon juice, bay leaves, salt and peppercorns in a saucepan. Heat to 205 to 210 degrees, about a low boil; drain. Remove and discard the bay leaves. Place the shrimp in an ice water bath for 5 minutes to stop the cooking. Remove from the water and cut into halves lengthwise. Combine with the honey and sambal in a small bowl; mix well. Marinate in the refrigerator.

3 Soak each rice paper sheet in a shallow bowl of 100-degree water for 15 seconds on each side. Arrange into 4 wrappers by placing 2 sheets for each wrapper in a slightly overlapping layer on a dry surface; let dry slightly.

4 Layer a small amount of lettuce, mango, mint, basil and 4 shrimp halves at the edge of each wrapper. Roll tightly to enclose the filling, tucking in the sides. Brush the last edge with cold water and press to seal.

5 Place on a plate and cover with a damp towel. Store in the refrigerator for up to 2 days. Slice each roll diagonally into 8 pieces. Serve with the dipping sauce.

Yields 16 (2-piece) servings

Cal-a-Vie High Fiber Seed Bread

1 Pour the boiling water over the bulgur in a small heatproof bowl. Let stand until cool. Mix the yeast with 3 cups warm water in a large mixing bowl and let stand for 5 minutes. Add the molasses, honey and canola oil and let stand for 5 minutes longer or until frothy.

2 Stir in the oat bran, wheat bran, poppy seeds, sesame seeds, sunflower seeds and salt. Add the cooled bulgur with any unabsorbed water. Add 7 cups of the flour and mix to form a stiff dough, mixing well. Knead lightly in the bowl, kneading in the remaining flour as needed.

3 Shape into a ball and place in an oiled bowl, turning to coat the surface. Cover with a towel and place in a warm place. Let stand for 1 hour or until doubled in bulk. Punch down the dough and knead on a floured surface for 5 to 7 minutes or until smooth and elastic.

4 Shape into 4 equal portions and pat into rectangles. Roll tightly to form loaves, pinching the seams to seal. Place in 4 oiled 9-inch loaf pans. Let rise in a warm place for 1 1/2 to 2 hours or until doubled in bulk.

5 Preheat the oven to 350 degrees. Bake the loaves for 45 to 50 minutes or until they sound hollow when tapped. Remove to a wire rack to cool completely. Cut each loaf into 16 slices. You may freeze these loaves, but you should slice them before freezing.

Yields 64 slices

2 cups boiling water

1 cup bulgur

2 tablespoons dry yeast

3 cups warm water

1 cup molasses

1/4 cup honey

1/2 cup canola oil

2 cups oat bran

2 cups wheat bran

1 cup poppy seeds

1 cup sesame seeds

1 cup sunflower seeds

1 1/2 teaspoons salt

8 1/2 to 9 cups flour

nutrition per serving						
CAL	CARB	PRO	FAT	FIBER	CHOL	SOD
122	17g	4g	5g	3g	0mg	58mg

guests' favorites

Fresh Corn and Yellow Summer Squash Soup

4 large ears of yellow or white corn

8 small to medium yellow crookneck
    summer squash

2 tablespoons minced shallot

1 tablespoon minced garlic

1 tablespoon olive oil

1/2 cup sake

4 cups vegetable stock or chicken stock

1 teaspoon hot red pepper sauce

juice of 1/2 lemon

1 tablespoon chopped fresh tarragon

3 tablespoons chopped fresh parsley or
    cilantro, for garnish

1 Cut the kernels from the ears of corn, discarding the cobs. Cut the squash into halves lengthwise and grill until tender. Cut into small pieces.

2 Sauté the shallot and garlic in the olive oil in a saucepan. Add the sake and cook until the alcohol cooks off. Add the stock and corn kernels. Bring to a low boil and cook for 15 minutes or until the corn is tender.

3 Process the corn and stock mixture in a blender until smooth. Return to the saucepan and add the squash, hot sauce, lemon juice and tarragon. Simmer for 15 minutes. Ladle into soup bowls and garnish with the chopped parsley or cilantro.

Yields 12 servings

nutrition per serving

CAL	CARB	PRO	FAT	FIBER	CHOL	SOD
83	16g	3g	2g	3g	0mg	171mg

Stuffed Tomato Salad

4 Roma tomatoes

1/4 cup whole wheat bread crumbs

4 teaspoons grated Romano cheese

1 1/2 tablespoons chopped basil

1 1/2 tablespoons chopped parsley

1/4 teaspoon pepper

2 teaspoons olive oil

2 cups fresh spinach

2 tablespoons Balsamic Vinaigrette
    (page 157)

1 Preheat the oven to 350 degrees. Cut the tomatoes into halves crosswise and place cut side up on a baking sheet.

2 Mix the bread crumbs, cheese, basil, parsley, pepper and olive oil in a bowl. Sprinkle the mixture over the tomatoes. Bake for 15 minutes or until the topping is golden brown. Serve on a bed of spinach and drizzle with the Balsamic Vinaigrette.

Yields 4 servings

nutrition per serving

CAL	CARB	PRO	FAT	FIBER	CHOL	SOD
83	9g	3g	5g	2g	2mg	430mg

Prentiss Prawns with Mango, Papaya and Grapefruit Salad

1 For the prawns, combine the soy sauce, apple juice, lime juice, sesame oil, honey, garlic and ginger in a bowl and mix well. Add the prawns and marinate for 30 minutes. Sauté the prawns in the marinade in a sauté pan until cooked through. Chill in the refrigerator.

2 For the vinaigrette, combine the balsamic vinegar, olive oil, herbs, salt and pepper in a bowl and mix well.

3 For the salad, combine the mango, papaya, grapefruit and tomatoes in a bowl and mix well. Add the vinaigrette and mix gently. Spoon the salad into wine glasses and arrange the prawns around the rims of the glasses.

Yields 6 servings

Prawns

3 tablespoons low-sodium soy sauce

1/2 cup apple juice

1/3 cup lime juice

1 tablespoon sesame oil

1 teaspoon honey

3 garlic cloves, crushed

1/4 cup minced fresh ginger

24 prawns, peeled and deveined

Balsamic Vinaigrette

2 tablespoons balsamic vinegar

2 tablespoons olive oil

2 tablespoons chopped herbs, such as
   parsley, basil, cilantro or chives

salt and pepper to taste

Salad

1 mango, chopped

1 papaya, chopped

1/2 grapefruit, sectioned

2 tomatoes, peeled, seeded and finely
   chopped

nutrition per serving						
CAL	CARB	PRO	FAT	FIBER	CHOL	SOD
282	27g	27g	8g	4g	175mg	500mg

guests' favorites

Wild Mushroom and Lobster Strudel

1 pound lobster or shrimp

1 tablespoon chopped shallot

1 teaspoon chopped garlic

1 tablespoon olive oil

1/2 cup quartered crimini mushrooms

1/3 cup sliced oyster mushrooms

1/2 cup chopped red bell pepper

4 scallions, thinly sliced

2 tablespoons chopped fresh tarragon

4 sheets frozen phyllo dough, thawed

8 ounces French-style green beans,
    cooked

8 pieces baby yellow summer
    squash, cooked

1 teaspoon toasted paprika, for garnish

4 pieces lobster mushrooms,
    for garnish (optional)

lobster claws, for garnish

4 sprigs fresh tarragon, for garnish

6 ounces Lobster Sauce (page 159)

nutrition per serving

CAL	CARB	PRO	FAT	FIBER	CHOL	SOD
264	25g	26g	7g	5g	108mg	689mg

1   Preheat the oven to 350 degrees. Sauté the lobster with the shallot and garlic in the olive oil in a saucepan for 1 minute. Add the mushrooms, bell pepper, scallions and tarragon. Cover and cook for 3 minutes. Let cool for several minutes.

2   Fold one sheet of the phyllo dough into quarters and spray with butter-flavor or olive oil nonstick cooking spray. Spoon 1/4 of the lobster mixture along 1 edge of the dough and roll to enclose the filling. Repeat with the remaining phyllo dough sheets and lobster mixture.

3   Place the strudels on a baking sheet and bake for 15 minutes or until golden brown. Serve with the green beans and summer squash. Garnish the plates with the toasted paprika, lobster mushrooms, lobster claws and tarragon; drizzle each serving with 1 ounce Lobster Sauce.

Yields 4 servings

Lobster Sauce

1 Sauté the lobster shells with the onion, carrot and celery in the olive oil in a saucepan for 1 minute. Add the wine and bring to a boil. Cook until the alcohol evaporates, then add the tomato paste, stock, bay leaf and tarragon. Cook until reduced by half.

2 Strain the mixture and season with salt and pepper. For a thicker sauce, stir in a slurry of arrowroot and stock and cook until thickened, stirring constantly.

Yields 8 (1-ounce) servings

2 lobster shells, rinsed

1/2 onion, coarsely chopped

1 carrot, coarsely chopped

1 rib celery, coarsely chopped

1 teaspoon olive oil

1/2 cup white wine

1 tablespoon tomato paste

3/4 cup chicken stock or vegetable stock

1 bay leaf

1 sprig tarragon

salt and pepper to taste

nutrition per serving

CAL	CARB	PRO	FAT	FIBER	CHOL	SOD
15	2g	<1g	1g	2g	0mg	90mg

Revitalizer

1 Combine the tomato juice cocktail, water, vegetables, tomatoes, celery, carrot, parsley, bay leaves, basil, rosemary, fennel seeds and red pepper in a large non-reactive saucepan. Bring to a boil. Reduce the heat to low and simmer for 40 minutes, stirring occasionally.

2 Press the mixture through a strainer set over a bowl using a wooden spoon to extract the juices, or process the mixture through a food mill. Discard the pulp.

3 Serve hot or cold. You may freeze the mixture in 1 cup amounts for later use. We do not recommend using any vegetables in the cabbage family as they impart a strong flavor.

4 You may substitute 1 tablespoon dried basil for the fresh basil and 1 teaspoon dried rosemary for the fresh rosemary.

Yields 10 (1-cup) servings

1 (48-ounce) bottle low-sodium tomato juice cocktail

3 cups filtered water

2 cups assorted sliced vegetables (such as root vegetables, onions and bell peppers)

4 tomatoes, chopped

2 ribs celery, chopped

1 large carrot, chopped

1 bunch parsley

2 bay leaves

2 tablespoons chopped fresh basil

2 teaspoons fresh rosemary

1/2 teaspoon fennel seeds

1/2 teaspoon crushed hot red pepper, or to taste

nutrition per serving

CAL	CARB	PRO	FAT	FIBER	CHOL	SOD
35	8g	2g	<1g	2g	0mg	80mg

guests' favorites

Fish and Shrimp en Papillote

4 (3-ounce) flounder fillets

16 (16- to 20-count) jumbo shrimp, peeled
    and butterflied

1 teaspoon Creole seasoning

4 ounces fresh spinach, julienned

4 ounces mixed red, yellow and green bell
    pepper rings

4 ounces wild mushrooms

8 ($1/4$-inch) slices Creole tomato

4 garlic cloves, roasted

kosher salt and cracked pepper to taste

6 ounces Herb Velouté (below)

8 green onions, sliced into 3-inch pieces,
    for garnish

1   Preheat the oven to 400 degrees. Sprinkle the fish and shrimp with Creole seasoning. Spray an 18×26-inch sheet of baking parchment with nonstick cooking spray. Arrange half the spinach, half the bell pepper, half the mushrooms, half the tomato and half the garlic on $1/2$ of the parchment; sprinkle with kosher salt and cracked pepper.

2   Place the fish and shrimp on top of the vegetables and sprinkle the remaining vegetables over and around the fish and shrimp. Drizzle with $11/2$ ounces of the Herb Velouté. Fold the parchment over to enclose the seafood and vegetables and seal by folding the edge over in tight overlapping folds.

3   Place the packet on a baking sheet and bake for 20 to 25 minutes. Remove to a serving platter and open the packet to serve "en papillote" or remove to individual serving plates. Garnish with the green onions.

Yields 4 servings

160

nutrition per serving						
CAL	CARB	PRO	FAT	FIBER	CHOL	SOD
139	13g	16g	1g	3g	16mg	734mg

Herb Velouté

3 cups low-sodium fish broth or bouillon

1 cup clam juice

$1/2$ cup dry vermouth

$11/2$ ounces arrowroot

1 cup evaporated skim milk

3 tablespoons chopped fresh chives

$21/2$ tablespoons chopped fresh basil

$21/2$ tablespoons chopped fresh tarragon

salt and pepper to taste

1   Bring the broth, clam juice and vermouth to a boil in a small saucepan. Make a thick paste of the arrowroot and a small amount of water in a cup.

2   Add the paste and the evaporated skim milk to the saucepan and return to a boil, stirring constantly. Stir in the chives, basil and tarragon and season with salt and pepper.

Yields 1 quart

Swiss Chard-Wrapped Halibut

1 Blanch the chard and remove the stems. Drizzle the lemon juice over the fish and season with salt and pepper. Place on the chard leaves and wrap to enclose the fish.

2 Place in the basket of a steamer and steam over boiling water for 10 minutes or until tender. Drizzle the Saffron Sauce over the fish. Serve with the rice and steamed vegetables.

Yields 4 servings

4 large red or green Swiss chard leaves

juice of 1 lemon

4 (3-ounce) fresh halibut fillets

salt and pepper to taste

Saffron Sauce (below)

1 cup cooked basmati rice

3 or 4 cups steamed vegetables

nutrition per serving						
CAL	CARB	PRO	FAT	FIBER	CHOL	SOD
235	23g	23g	5g	4g	35mg	410mg

Saffron Sauce

1 Combine the wine, water, broth base, shallot, olive oil, honey, white pepper and saffron in a small saucepan. Bring the mixture to a boil.

2 Reduce the heat and simmer for 5 minutes, stirring frequently. Add the arrowroot and cook until thickened, stirring constantly.

Yields 5 (2-ounce) servings

$1/2$ cup dry white wine

$1/4$ cup water

4 ounces Eastern Foods low-sodium
   Chicken Broth Base

1 tablespoon chopped fresh shallot

1 teaspoon olive oil

1 teaspoon honey

$1/4$ teaspoon white pepper

$1/4$ teaspoon saffron

1 teaspoon arrowroot

nutrition per serving						
CAL	CARB	PRO	FAT	FIBER	CHOL	SOD
80	4g	2g	5g	<1g	0mg	2687mg

guests' favorites

Mild Vegetarian Enchiladas with Carrot Sauce

Carrot Sauce

2 large or 5 medium carrots, chopped

1 onion, chopped

2/3 cup chopped celery (about 2 ribs)

1 garlic clove, mashed

1 tablespoon cumin

1 tablespoon coriander

1 teaspoon dried oregano, or 1 tablespoon
   chopped fresh oregano

1 teaspoon ground cinnamon

2 tablespoons chili powder

3 cups low-sodium tomato juice cocktail
   or Revitalizer (page 159)

Enchiladas

2 teaspoons olive oil

1 teaspoon each cumin, coriander and
   chili powder

1 teaspoon dried basil, or 1 tablespoon
   chopped fresh basil

1/2 teaspoon sea salt

1/4 teaspoon pepper

1/2 red bell pepper, chopped

1 cup chopped zucchini

1 cup chopped yellow squash

1 cup chopped carrot

8 ounces crimini mushrooms, chopped

1 garlic clove, minced

1 cup cooked black beans

6 whole wheat tortillas

3 ounces Monterey Jack cheese, shredded

6 sprigs fresh cilantro, for garnish

1   For the sauce, combine the carrots, onion, celery and garlic in a saucepan. Add the cumin, coriander, oregano, cinnamon, chili powder and tomato juice cocktail. Bring to a boil and reduce the heat. Simmer for 20 minutes or until the vegetables are tender, stirring occasionally. Process the mixture in several batches in a blender until puréed. Combine in a saucepan and keep warm.

2   For the enchiladas, heat the olive oil in a large nonstick skillet and add the cumin, coriander, chili powder, basil, sea salt and pepper. Cook for 1 minute. Add the bell pepper, zucchini, squash, carrot, mushrooms and garlic. Cook for 15 minutes or until the vegetables are tender-crisp, stirring frequently. Stir in the black beans.

3   Preheat the oven to 350 degrees. Spoon 2 cups of the sauce into a smaller saucepan. Dip 1 tortilla at a time into the 2 cups sauce, shaking off the excess; place on a work surface. Spoon 1/6 of the vegetable mixture onto each tortilla and roll to enclose the filling. Place seam side down in a baking pan.

4   Ladle the remaining enchilada sauce over the enchiladas and sprinkle with the cheese. Bake for 5 minutes. Garnish with fresh cilantro.

5   You may chop the vegetables by hand or pulse in a food processor to cut into small uniform chunks. You may assemble the enchiladas with cold ingredients prepared in advance. Bake them for 10 minutes before sprinkling with the cheese and then bake for 5 minutes longer to melt the cheese.

Yields 6 servings

guests' favorites

nutrition per serving						
CAL	CARB	PRO	FAT	FIBER	CHOL	SOD
245	45g	14g	5g	8g	10mg	700mg

Basil Spaghettini in Tomato Concassée

1 Cut an X in the bottoms of the tomatoes and blanch in boiling water in a large saucepan for about 2 minutes or until the skin can be easily removed. Peel, seed and process the tomatoes in a blender or food processor until puréed.

2 Sauté the onions and garlic in the olive oil in a saucepan over low heat for about 5 minutes. Add the wine, mushrooms, tomato purée, oregano, basil, fennel, salt and pepper. Simmer for 30 minutes. Add the tomato paste and simmer for 10 minutes longer.

3 Cook the pasta al dente in water in a saucepan; drain. Spoon onto serving plates and top with the tomato concassée and cheese. Serve with grilled asparagus.

Yields 6 servings

12 ripe tomatoes

2 onions, chopped

1 tablespoon minced garlic

1 tablespoon olive oil

1/2 cup red wine

1 pound crimini or porcini
   mushrooms, sliced

1 tablespoon chopped fresh oregano

1 tablespoon chopped fresh basil

1 teaspoon ground fennel

1/2 teaspoon salt, or to taste

1/2 teaspoon freshly ground pepper, or
   to taste

2 tablespoons tomato paste

16 ounces dry basil spaghettini, spaghetti
   or angel hair pasta

1/4 cup grated Parmesan cheese

nutrition per serving						
CAL	CARB	PRO	FAT	FIBER	CHOL	SOD
407	85g	17g	6g	10g	3mg	276mg

163

Havens Spa Génoise

1 Combine the eggs, egg whites, sugar, cardamom, nutmeg and lemon zest in a double boiler and mix well. Heat to 120 degrees over simmering water. Remove from the heat and beat until tripled in volume.

2 Preheat the oven to 350 degrees. Cool the egg mixture to room temperature and stir in the vanilla. Fold in the flour. Spread in a baking pan lined with baking parchment. Bake for 15 minutes.

Yields 16 servings

10 eggs

2 egg whites

1 1/2 cups sugar or Splenda

1/4 teaspoon cardamom

1/2 teaspoon nutmeg

2 teaspoons grated lemon zest

2 teaspoons vanilla extract

2 cups unbleached flour

nutrition per serving						
CAL	CARB	PRO	FAT	FIBER	CHOL	SOD
185	32g	6g	3g	<1g	132mg	51mg

guests' favorites

Brownies

4 egg whites

1/2 cup honey

1/2 cup packed brown sugar

1/2 cup applesauce

1/4 cup water

1 tablespoon Kahlúa

1/2 cup dried fruit, such as pears, apricots
   or pitted cherries

2/3 cup baking cocoa

1/2 teaspoon baking powder

2 1/4 cups whole wheat pastry flour

1/2 cup chopped walnuts

1 Preheat the oven to 350 degrees. Combine the egg whites, honey, brown sugar, applesauce, water, Kahlúa and dried fruit in a blender. Process until smooth.

2 Sift the baking cocoa and baking powder into a large bowl. Add the flour and walnuts. Stir in the fruit mixture and mix until moistened.

3 Spoon into two 9-inch pie plates sprayed with nonstick cooking oil. Bake for 35 minutes.

Yields 32 servings

nutrition per serving						
CAL	CARB	PRO	FAT	FIBER	CHOL	SOD
79	16g	2g	2g	2g	0mg	17mg

Cal-a-Vie Tea Recipes

1 Combine all the ingredients for each tea with 32 ounces of water in a large saucepan and bring to a boil.

2 Remove from the heat and let steep for several minutes. Strain and serve hot or iced.

Yields 15 servings

Strawberry Guavazinger Tea

16 ounces strawberry guava juice

16 ounce apricot nectar

4 chamomile tea bags

4 red zinger tea bags

1 banana, mashed

2 tablespoons honey

nutrition per serving						
CAL	CARB	PRO	FAT	FIBER	CHOL	SOD
48	13g	<1g	<1g	<1g	0mg	7mg

Sleepy Peachy Mango Tea

32 ounces mango peach juice

4 lemon zinger tea bags

4 sleepy time tea bags

2 tablespoons honey

6 whole cloves

juice of 1 lemon

nutrition per serving						
CAL	CARB	PRO	FAT	FIBER	CHOL	SOD
39	10g	<1g	<1g	<1g	0mg	9mg

Cal-a-Vie Tea Recipes

Hibiscus Cooler Tea

32 ounces hibiscus cooler juice

4 red zinger tea bags

4 sunburst tea bags

juice of 1 lemon

2 tablespoons honey

nutrition per serving

CAL	CARB	PRO	FAT	FIBER	CHOL	SOD
38	10g	<1g	<1g	<1g	0mg	2mg

Wild Forest Blackberry Tea

32 ounces papaya nectar

4 wild forest blackberry tea bags

4 mandarin orange spice tea bags

1 banana, mashed

2 tablespoons honey

nutrition per serving

CAL	CARB	PRO	FAT	FIBER	CHOL	SOD
50	13g	<1g	<1g	1g	0mg	3mg

Cranraspberry Cove Tea

32 ounces cranberry-raspberry juice

3 cranberry cove tea bags

3 mandarin orange spice tea bags

3 wild forest blackberry tea bags

juice of 1/2 lime

6 whole cloves

2 tablespoons honey

nutrition per serving

CAL	CARB	PRO	FAT	FIBER	CHOL	SOD
52	14g	<1g	<1g	<1g	0mg	2mg

Papaya Nectar Tea

32 ounces papaya nectar

8 cinnamon apple tea bags

1 banana, mashed

juice of 1/2 lemon

juice of 1/2 orange

8 whole cloves

2 tablespoons honey (optional)

nutrition per serving

CAL	CARB	PRO	FAT	FIBER	CHOL	SOD
54	14g	<1g	<1g	1g	0mg	4mg

Pineapple Sunburst Tea

32 ounces pineapple juice

4 mandarin orange tea bags

4 sunburst tea bags

juice of 1 orange

2 tablespoons honey

nutrition per serving

CAL	CARB	PRO	FAT	FIBER	CHOL	SOD
47	12g	<1g	<1g	<1g	0mg	1mg

Cinnamon Almond Sunset Tea

32 ounces apple juice

4 almond sunset tea bags

4 chamomile tea bags

2 red zinger tea bags

1 banana, mashed

juice of 1 orange

2 cinnamon sticks

2 tablespoons honey

nutrition per serving

CAL	CARB	PRO	FAT	FIBER	CHOL	SOD
52	13g	<1g	<1g	1g	0mg	2mg

guests' favorites

nutritional information

The nutritional analysis for these recipes is computed from information obtained from many resources, including information supplied by the United States Department of Agriculture, computer databases, nutrition/health journals, and ESHA Research, a nutrition and fitness software program.

A few specialty items, new products, and some processed foods may not have been available from these resources so a product as close to the listed recipe ingredient was used for analysis or an average of the values of similar food products was used. For specific nutritional information, read the label on the individual package or product.

U.S. standardized measures were used and unless specified differently, all ingredients were measured as level.

The following information may be helpful in the home preparation of the recipes:

⚜ Flour is unsifted all-purpose flour.

⚜ Eggs are large.

⚜ Garnishes were not analyzed in the nutritional profile.

⚜ Low-fat milk is 1% milk fat.

⚜ Olive oil was used for oil.

⚜ Alcohol ingredients were analyzed as basic ingredients, cooking can reduce the amount of alcohol due to evaporation, thus decreasing the calorie number.

⚜ Artificial sweeteners should be used with care, following the package directions; prolonged heat changes the taste of many of these products. The recipes were analyzed using honey or sugar unless otherwise specified.

nutrients

Proper nutrition is a key component for good health and physical fitness. For weight trainers, proper nutrition consumption is the most important aid for making gains. An appropriate assortment of foods from the food groups can provide all of the basic nutrients needed for the body to function at an optimal level. Food satisfies three basic bodily needs, (1) the need for energy, (2) the need for new tissue growth and repair, (3) the need for energy regulation of metabolic functions.

Water

The most essential of all nutrients—no caloric value—necessary for energy production. Drinking a minimum of 8 to 10 glasses of water per day helps your liver do the job of metabolizing fat and detoxifying your body. When you drink too much juice, coffee, soda, and not enough water, your liver has to metabolize that stuff, compromising its fat wasting effectiveness. In addition, drinking enough water aides in controlling your weight and appetite, regulating your body temperature, and balancing your bodily fluids. Remember, our body composition is made of 50% water, and our muscles are 70% water, so don't neglect this simple method to enhance our body's overall wellness.

How much water should you drink each day? Activity and environmental conditions are the two most important factors that determine your body's need for water. During study, rest, and sleep, the loss of water is much less from the body than during strenuous activities, such as training. When the temperature is hot and the humidity is low, more water evaporates from your body's surface.

In sedentary individuals, thirst is an adequate signal of the needs of the body. But with serious athletes, and all people using high intensity training, the desire for water is not an adequate indication of the body's requirements.

Minerals

Minerals are inorganic compounds (they don't contain carbon) that serve a variety of functions in the body. Some, such as calcium and phosphorus, are used to build bones and teeth. Others are important components of hormones, such as iodine in thyroxine. Iron is essential for the formation of hemoglobin, the oxygen-carrier within red blood cells.

Certain minerals called electrolytes help regulate muscle contraction, conduction of nerve impulses, and regulation of normal heart rhythm.

Minerals are classified into two groups, based on the body's need. Major minerals are needed in amounts greater than 100 mg per day. Calcium, phosphorus, magnesium, sodium, and chloride fall into this category. Minor minerals, or trace elements, are needed in amounts less than 100 mg per day. Iron, zinc, selenium, copper, and iodine are minor minerals.

Vitamins

Vitamins are organic (carbon-containing) compounds that the body requires in minute amounts but cannot manufacture. Vitamins provide no calories and cannot be used as fuel. Instead, they function as metabolic regulators that govern the processes of energy production, growth, maintenance, and repair. Thirteen vitamins have been identified. Each has a special function in the body and also works in complicated ways with other nutrients. Vitamins are divided into two groups: water soluble and fat soluble. Vitamin C and the B complex vitamins are soluble in water. Excess water-soluble vitamins are excreted, mainly in the urine, and have to be replaced on a regular basis. However, excessive consumption of such water-soluble vitamins as niacin, B6, and C can also produce serious side effects.

Fat-soluble vitamins include A, D, E, and K, which are stored in the body fat, principally in the liver. The solubility characteristic is important in determining whether the body can store the vitamin. Taking a greater amount of fat-soluble vitamins than the body needs over a significant period can produce serious toxic effects. While vitamin A is found only in meat, dark orange-yellow and green leafy plants contain substances called carotenes that the body can convert to vitamin A. Unlike vitamin A, carotenes are fairly safe when consumed in large quantities. The body stores excesses of carotenes (which can make the skin look yellow-orange) rather than converting them to vitamin A.

Protein

Protein is a major structural component of all body tissues and is required for all tissue growth and repair. Proteins are also necessary components of hormones, enzymes, and blood-plasma transport systems. Protein is not a significant energy source during rest or exercise. However, the body will use protein for energy when calorie or carbohydrate intake is inadequate (during fasting or a low-carbohydrate diet).

The proteins in both plant and animal sources are composed of the same basic units called amino acids. Of the more than twenty amino acids that have been identified, nine must be provided by our diet and are called essential amino acids. Meat, fish, and poultry contain all nine essential amino acids and are called complete proteins. Vegetable proteins, such as beans and grains, are called incomplete proteins because they do not supply all of the essential amino acids.

However, the body can make complete proteins if a variety of plant foods—beans, grains, vegetables, nuts, and seeds—and sufficient calories are eaten during the day. Vegetarians don't need to worry about combining specific foods within a meal to achieve complete proteins, since the body will utilize amino acids from foods eaten at different meals. Well-balanced vegetarian diets may even decrease the risk of heart disease and cancer, because they are lower in fat and higher in complex carbohydrates than the average American diet.

Fat

Kilocalories (kcal) are the units by which energy is measured when referring to the energy taken in by food and expended with exercise. Fats are the most concentrated source of food energy. One gram of fat supplies about 9 kcal, compared to the 4 kcal supplied by carbohydrates and protein.

Fats are the body's only source of the fatty acid called linoleic acid that is essential for growth and skin maintenance. Fat insulates and protects the body's organs against trauma and exposure to cold and is involved in the absorption and transport of the fat-soluble vitamins.

Fats are the source of fatty acids, which are divided into two categories: saturated and unsaturated (including monounsaturated and polyunsaturated fatty acids). These fatty acids differ from each other chemically based on the nature of the bond between carbon and hydrogen atoms.

As a general rule, saturated fat is solid at room temperature and is derived mainly from animal sources. Unsaturated fat is liquid at room temperature and is found mainly in plants. Monounsaturated and polyunsaturated fats should be emphasized, since they tend to lower the blood cholesterol level. Saturated fats tend to raise the level of blood cholesterol and high blood cholesterol levels are associated with an increased risk of coronary heart disease.

Carbohydrates

Carbohydrates such as starch and sugar are the most readily available source of food energy. During digestion and metabolism, all carbohydrates are broken down to a simple sugar called glucose for use as the body's principal energy source. Glucose is stored in the liver and muscle tissue as glycogen. A carbohydrate-rich diet is necessary to maintain muscle glycogen, the preferred fuel for most types of exercise.

Sugar and complex carbohydrates (starch) are grouped together because they have a chemical similarity. All carbohydrates are made up of one or more simple sugars, the most common being glucose, fructose, and galactose. The simple sugar glucose connected to the simple sugar fructose forms sucrose, or table sugar. Complex carbohydrates contain anywhere from 300 to 1,000 glucose units hooked together. The body uses both starches and sugars for energy.

Although the body uses both the sugars and starches for energy, a high-performance diet emphasizes complex carbohydrates. Foods high in complex carbohydrates, such as bread, cereal, rice, beans, pasta, and vegetables also supply other nutrients such as vitamins, minerals, and fibers. Some sweet foods that are high in sugar (e.g., candy bars, cookies, and donuts) supply carbohydrates but also contain a high amount of fat and only insignificant amounts of vitamins and minerals.

Fruit contains the sweetest of all simple sugars—fructose. Since fruit is mostly water, its sugar and calorie content is relatively low. Like starchy foods, most fruits are rich in nutrients and virtually fat-free.

index

index

index

index

Cal-a-Vie
LIVING
gourmet spa cuisine

Cal-a-Vie
LIVING
gourmet spa cuisine

Please send copies to:

Name _____

Address _____

City _____ State _____ Zip_____

Phone _____

Quantity	Price	Total
_____	$34.95	$ _____

CA Residents add $2.71 tax per book $ _____

Shipping & Handling $4.95 per book $ _____

Call for shipping charges on quantity purchases

Total enclosed $ _____

All inquiries and orders should be addressed to:

Phone orders accepted.

Please do not send cash.

Sorry, no COD orders.

Please make checks payable to:

Cal-a-Vie Spa

Please charge my: ☐ Visa   ☐ MasterCard   ☐ AmEx

Account#_____

Expiration Date: _____

Cardholder's Signature: _____

Cal-a-Vie Health Spa
29402 Spa Havens Way
Vista, CA 92084
1-866-SPA-HAVENS
www.cal-a-vie.com